THE BARTER WAY
TO BEAT INFLATION

Other books by George W. Burtt:

Putting Yourself Across with the Art of Graphic Persuasion
Stop Crying at Your Own Movies
The Explicated Tao
The Vector Handbook
Psychographics in Personal Growth

THE BARTER WAY
TO BEAT INFLATION

George W. Burtt

EVEREST HOUSE
Publishers   *New York*

Library of Congress Cataloging in Publication Data:
Burtt, George W., 1914–
  The barter way to beat inflation.
  1. Barter. I. Title.
HG230.7.B87   1980   332.5'5   79-28094
ISBN: 0-89696-053-6

Published simultaneously in Canada by
Beaverbooks, Pickering, Ontario
Manufactured in the United States of America

Designed by Joyce Cameron Weston
First Edition   F G

Table of Contents

The propensity to truck, barter, and exchange is common to all men. —Adam Smith

Introduction

THIS BOOK IS WRITTEN to give you the inside attitudes, angles, and approaches which make for success in trading.

Are you employed? Don't give up your job. Begin to barter as you are. Do you have a business? Are you a professional man? You don't have to sacrifice any cash customers or present clients in order to benefit from barter. Trading adds to cash; it does not replace it.

What barter can do *for you* depends on how well you absorb and then apply the simple trading techniques spelled out in this book.

But there is no question about what bartering has done *for me*—and it has done even more for others of my acquaintance. In terms of things and services, here are some of the bartered acquisitions I have made during the past year alone:

Office equipment I have obtained by barter include a printing calculator (electronic), a hand calculator, an adding machine, a telephone answering device. (Had I needed more office gear I could have traded for it.)

Office services which have been supplied to me through trading

7

form quite a roster: advertising, printing, typesetting, secretarial and notarial services, photography and color photo prints, automobile tune-up and body repair, legal services, CPA accounting, bookkeeping, stationery, art materials, janitorial services, flowers, food and beverages and catering.

For my personal use you can add to the previous list such items as magazine subscriptions, formal wear rental, watches, jewelry, hotel and motel accommodations; medical, dental and chiropractic services; veterinary services.

In addition I obtained by bartering men's and women's clothing, shoes, vitamins, prescriptions and other drug-store merchandise, baby togs and playthings, cleaning, carpeting, smoking materials, restaurant and bar service . . .

I could go on, but you get the idea. Virtually everything that a person needs to live can be provided *without payment of cash* by barter. The only exceptions may be taxes, utilities, postage, and payments on cash debts you already owe. But even these can sometimes be arranged through barter.

In addition to things and services, learning to be a trader has given me many valuable personal assets. It can do the same for you. Barter has taught me—and it can teach you—to be more independent and self-reliant.

Trading sharpens your creative capabilities. It trains you to keep your attention on essentials, such as things and services, rather than on their substitutes, money and credit.

More than this, bartering trains you so you get out of debt and stay that way. In trading you learn to develop surpluses instead of deficits. You tend to have more than you need rather than less.

If any of this excites your interest, then make this book truly your own by studying it. Absorb the handful of basic ideas it expounds. Apply them in your own places of livelihood. You'll add both the pleasure and profit of trading.

Good luck!

THE BARTER WAY
TO BEAT INFLATION

The greatest meliorator of the world is selfish, hucksterina trade. —*Ralph Waldo Emerson*

CHAPTER 1

How to Forecast Your Own Successful Trading Career

You, LIKE ME AND THE REST OF HUMANITY, are engaged night and day, waking and sleeping, in an ongoing trading process.

Being part of nature ourselves, we reflect it in our actions. We exchange air, twenty times a minute or so, around the clock. Food and liquids enter our bodies, are modified, and pass along. On a larger scale, our tilling and harvesting, mining and garnering, take from the rest of nature for our human purposes. After conversion to our use, these natural things cycle back into outer nature again.

Between ourselves, in our social and business relationships we are engaged in exchanges at another level. An untrained eye can note when a grain field has been harvested. It takes a more educated observer to see and evaluate the transaction involved between two adults in some meaningful interpersonal exchange—a barter deal of a sort.

Yet these exchanges can and do affect our lives markedly.

And our built-in attitudes determine whether we are "seller" or "buyer" in such encounters; that is, whether we or the other person involved gets things the way we want them.

I have no intention of writing a philosophical treatise, or a study in applied psychology.

However, it is necessary to grasp what is really going on in the exchange process in general if you wish to be able to use it for your own benefit in specific instances.

Let's narrow our field. We are discussing the exchange of things of general human utility. "Things" also includes services and other intangibles as well as items we can see, taste, hear, smell, or touch.

Figure 1 shows a handy way to conceptualize how we get—and get rid of—things in our lives. It is a sort of spectrum of exchange.

Toward the left side of this range considerable effort—force—is involved. We expend this effort getting and keeping what we value. Law enforcement; armed forces: these terms describe how lawful authorities acquire or defend property or rights.

Living under a system of laws, we take our cue from them. We obtain or dispose of property and rights by lawful means, assured that force stands behind us to guarantee that justice is done. Or, conversely, if we are lawbreakers we employ force to obtain what we wish. Against these, as private citizens, we too may employ force legally in certain instances.

On the other side of the spectrum, little or no effort is needed. Desirable things or services are given or received without force being required, without payment demanded or exacted.

Transactions are going on continuously over the whole range we are discussing. We ourselves may be on either side of a given exchange, at any point on the spectrum. But only if we are free to be. Most of us, most of the time, are constrained by our beliefs and habits to operate in narrow portions of this total exchange spectrum.

Money is one such thin sliver of the whole potential.

Those who govern create money and money systems.

Those governed follow along the lines laid down for them.

Exchange Spectrum

	Legal Ownership
	Adverse Possession
	Eminent Domain
Exchange by	Seize by Force
Force	Steal/Burglarize
	Take by Threat
	Obtain by Fraud
	Acquire by Enticement
	More/less Equal Exchange
	Give Token Amount Only
Mutual Exchange	Symbolic Payment
	Promises (including credit)
	Get by Rational Argument
	Gifts Asked For
	Donations Unsought
Unforced Exchange	Natural Gifts (Air, Water, etc.)
	Unowned Natural Supply

Our working lives are bought with money.

We live in what behavioral psychologists call a "token economy." Such economies are also established in prisons and asylums. The captive members are rewarded for desired behavior with M & M candies.

M & M. $ & $.

The scale may be the main difference between the two systems.

Please don't misunderstand. I think money is fine. I like it, I welcome it, I spend it.

But money is only a fraction of the means by which exchanges of things can and do take place.

So let us free ourselves to use other methods besides money, especially since our whole money system seems to be in jeopardy.

Barter—the Shortcut Around Money

If you live in the city, the chances are that you have almost forgotten that barter exists.

Call it barter, or trading, or exchange, it means swapping one commodity or service for something else.

The suspiciousness of the typical big-city resident in our roiled melting-pots militates against trading with strangers. And who has neighbors in the metropolitan stewpots?

So bartering has almost vanished as part of city life over recent generations—except trading for money.

So, city-dweller, this entire subject may be a novel one for you. You will, I hope, study this book for your pleasure and to your benefit.

If you happen to live in a small town or a rural area, though, you have probably been trading all your life. A few things written here may be old stories, which you can top out of your own experience. Even so, you may learn some things of value about trading you never suspected.

Please keep checking back to that exchange spectrum in Figure 1 as you read these next few pages. You will catch on better that way to the examples I am going to give of trading *around* money to your advantage.

Professional fund-raisers and related entrepreneurial types use many of these methods on behalf of their clients or themselves.

For instance, the use of *enticement* in the form of desirable women has been a tactic of the unscrupulous to get what they want throughout the ages.

You'll find this point on the chart just to the left of center. You may not want to employ enticement yourself in order to arrange an exchange deal, but if so you'd be a very rare specimen.

Advertisers use enticement, via sex-object ladies in their ads, to lure customers to their products. (Of course, ladies themselves do a very good job of this, too, for their own purposes. But that is another subject.)

On the other side of center, is the *token payment.*

This ruse is almost like getting something free, if used right.

The dollar-a-year men who, in times of national emergency, head up big government projects or departments, have been bartered for in this way. The employing executives were saying to these executives, practically in so many words, that they were worth more than money could pay for.

The prestige of position, and the satisfaction of important work well done for the public good, were the real payment. The nominal $1.00 was merely to keep the record straight that they were, after all, *employees.*

Symbolic payment is just as good a stratagem.

It's not a bad deal for the institution, for instance, to award an honorary degree (a few words on a sheet of sheepskin presented with a suitable flourish) in exchange for a private library of rare books.

Nor is it too bad a deal to chisel a name on a cornerstone as the trade-off for the gift of the building itself.

And on a smaller scale, the donor's name on a bronze plaque is fair exchange for a hospital wing. So is the brass tag on every bed inside, each bearing the name of one of a host of lesser benefactors.

Even better, why not *just ask* for what you want?

A minister I knew in Los Angeles had a budget that ran into the hundreds of thousands of dollars. That in a time when a dollar was still worth eighty cents or so.

While the annual gigantic funding drive raised the bulk of this huge amount through the every-member-canvass technique used by the lay committee, there seemed always to be a hefty chunk left to pry loose from somewhere.

The pastor simply went directly to those who had the most. And asked for what was needed.

The budget figure was always met.

I am not going to bore you with further examples of persons able to barter along one exchange point or another on our scale. You can supply as many instances as you choose from your own knowledge of the world. Look for those able to get what they want without money.

Please keep two points in mind, though.

Some individuals are free to operate at levels on the spectrum in which force, stratagem, symbols, or sheer *chutzpah* are the essential elements. Or at points in between, or involving these in combinations.

And you and I, for whatever reasons of experience or ability, are frozen out of many of these operating modes.

We'll seek to open these clogged channels as we proceed.

Just What Does Make a Trader Tick?

As we've noted, some people are free to range across our scale or exchange and manage transactions most of us would not dare, or perhaps not even conceive possible.

In the sense that I'm using the term, these people are *traders*.

Although as individuals they differ from each other as much as other people, they share points in common.

The first of these is relative *freedom* to speak, move, act, arrange, carry out. More than most others, these trader types are self-possessed and self-actualized. They are able to operate simply as themselves, if that is suitable, or to align other individuals or organizations for their mutual purposes.

Traders are not only able to speak to and mingle with others but they also seem to enjoy doing so.

Still, good traders are not complete extroverts. They are also sufficiently introspective to articulate plans. They are sensitive enough to the realities of others to be able to work them into their approaches.

They are flexible. A good trader uses not just one or two standard formulas over and over, but adapts his tactics—and if need be, his strategy—to the situation at hand.

Successful traders have a neutral sense of self-worth. They are not too proud to plead, if that is necessary. They are not too noble to stoop to dirty work when required. Nor are they compulsively humble, apologetic, or self-effacing. They are not mired down in ego problems or matters of personal identity. They work out exchanges without letting their own personalities get in their way.

Such traders like what they are doing. They take great pleasure in getting good things for themselves, and in letting the benefits rub off on others involved with them.

They act according to their own judgment and conscience, not despite scruples they must overcome (that leads to ulcers) but because they have a wider view and deeper understanding than those who have a narrow set of guidelines for individual conduct. The petty hang-ups that limit the actions—and achievements— of most people simply do not exist in the personalities of good traders.

Skilled barterers I have observed operate with a bias built in, tilted in their own favor. They *expect* their offers to be accepted. They *intend* to make a profit, and a good one. They *know* their plans will be given the green light by whoever must approve them. *Of course* doors will open, and *naturally* they will be welcome wherever they go.

Good traders are also concerned about the satisfaction of the other parties in their exchanges. A trader of ability likes to set up enduring trade relationships (they assure steady profits with little work). To do this he must keep his partners happy too. In turn, this requires him to keep his own operation clean and his dealings fair.

Good traders are *independent*. They do not permanently sign on as employees of someone else. They are self-motivated, self-directed. They take on the identification of any other person or organization only briefly, if that is essential to carry out a project of their own.

Good traders are concerned, too, about keeping the environment serene, clean, and receptive to exchange. Hence they extend their personal practices as far as they can by example and preachment. They not only favor good business (and the moral and ethical standards that make it possible) but they also actively work to achieve such conditions through their organizing abilities and general understanding of what is needed.

Do you get from all this the sense that a good trader is above all else a good citizen? That is true, in my observation.

Our leading figures in business, the professions, education, science, government, religion all display at least some of these qualities.

The founders of our government, to a man, possessed and demonstrated them; yet they were not ostensibly engaged in trading or exchange at all.

In discussing traders and trading, we are really talking about human beings and how they operate.

The good trader—the broad-gauged human being trained in transactions—is really *homo superior*. Such a person is a forerunner of types who will be generally more numerous in our societies of the future.

You and I are not in training to become star-class citizens of this kind, of course. It is enough that we know what some of the principal ingredients are in the makeup of good traders. If we then incorporate a few significant factors observed in them, making them part of our own behavior, the results can astound our friends and amaze even us.

Three-Minute Test of Your Trading Attitudes

There is a general assumption in professional helping circles that attitudes are formed by us out of our assessment of our own life experience. Aptitudes, on the other hand, are thought to be innate—we are born with them.

The facts are not very clear. The line between the two sets of characteristics is arbitrarily drawn. Moreover, the educational, psychological, employment, and other spheres of human survey have more tests than they know how to deal with. None, to my knowledge, would be able to sort out just those qualities which together favor success in the field of barter.

	CHECK BOXES TO SCORE YOURSELF		
Attitude	*That's not me*	*Well, sometimes*	*Hey, right on!*
I enjoy challenges—new situations, people, things.			
I go after what I want if the goal is realistic.			
I like persuading people to see things my way.			
I prefer to make my own plans and decisions.			
I do things now, if at all feasible, not later, as a matter of policy.			

	CHECK BOXES TO SCORE YOURSELF		
Attitude	*That's not me*	*Well, sometimes*	*Hey, right on!*
I'm a bargain hunter and buy everyting I can at sales, closeouts.			
I buy several items of a kind at once to have a supply on hand.			
If I think something is priced too high I don't hesitate to bargain.			
I appreciate owning things, but I sell or give them easily.			
I value my time and possessions highly, but not overweeningly so.			
I take satisfaction in finding easier, shorter, better ways to do things.			

This Trading Attitudes test, and the Barter Aptitudes checklist which follows, are not meant to be definitive. But they will be *some* indicators of how you stack up against qualities I have noted in expert traders over the years.

If you wish to shift some items from one chart to the other, where in your judgment they fit better, please do so. Attitude, aptitude, what do names matter? It's the amount of certain kinds of personality factors that seems to be the important consideration.

If most of your answers should fall in the *That's Not Me* column, don't let it bother you. You may have other qualities or abilities not mentioned which more than compensate. Or you may develop such capabilities or attitudes as time goes on. If trading and barter interest you, by all means follow your instinct and continue to be active in exchanging.

More likely, you'll find the majority of your responses in the *Well, Sometimes* boxes. If so, that indicates you are blessed with a good portion of the attitudes I have observed at work in good traders I have known. Keep on trading, learning as you go. What this book can teach you, plus your own study and experience, may add polish to your natural ways of looking at the world and doing things so you become an even better barterer.

If a good many of your rating checks were in the *Hey, Right On!* column, you already demonstrate a lot of the attitudes good traders have. You can have a lot of fun—and success in trading— ahead of you.

Checklist of Your Barter Aptitudes

Beginning in the late 1920s with the work of Johnson O'Connor,[1] there has been much research done on human aptitudes. Quite accurate tests have been developed which pinpoint native talent for many kinds of human activity.

Dozens of specific tests can reveal whether you're likely to succeed in jobs requiring mathematics, finger dexterity, tweezer dexterity, tonal memory, and so on and on.

Barter is not a simple activity, and the test has yet to be con-

[1] In the late 1920s Johnson O'Connor established the Human Engineering Institute in Hoboken, New Jersey. He and his co-researchers devised many aptitude tests which were accurate in determining individual capabilities for such items as finger dexterity, manual dexterity, structural visualization (wiggly block tests), and even one test (called by HEI "Ideaphoria") for pinpointing persons unusually gifted in matters involving words and ideas.

structed which will show with great accuracy anyone's native gifts in that line. But some characteristics shown by people good at barter are likely to be present in the personal aptitudes of others with a potential to become experts in the field of exchange.

Hence the brief checklist that follows is not intended to be more than a general indication that you do or don't share qualities I have noted in the behavior of successful traders. As credit men know, the best guarantee that a person will be a good risk is a track record of prompt payments in the past. So too with barter-related matters. If you have been busily doing a number of things traders do—whether you have been a barterer or not—the indications are that you will continue to do them when actively exchanging in times to come.

Thus our checklist on page 23.

Grade yourself on each question from a 1 for "little or never" to a 5 for "that's almost always the case."

Then total your points.

A score that edges down below 20 will show that, at least on this rating scale, your present behavior doesn't reflect too many items noted in active traders. But even so, be of good cheer. Trade to your heart's content. You'll learn—and grow—as you go.

If you come out in the 20s or 30s, you should do well at barter if you apply yourself to it.

And if your score winds up greater than 40, you're practically a winner at trading already (according to my view) even if you've never officially done any exchanging at all.

If you'll reread the preceding section about what makes traders tick, you'll notice that so far as I am concerned good traders are good citizens who are active in exchange transaction. So the freer, broader, deeper, and more mature a human being you are, the more successful you will be at exchanges at all levels of life.

If you are outgoing, friendly, a good mixer, a wise counselor and such, that helps you to be a fuller human being as well as a better trader if you turn your hand to that. And if you are insight-

Aptitude	SCORE YOURSELF				
	1	2	3	4	5
Maybe I'm just lucky, but I always seem to find what I need when I want it.					
Without really trying, I find myself seeing new or different uses for existing things.					
I'm blessed with plenty of energy and can keep on a project after most others have given up.					
People are repeatedly asking my advice and take my counsel seriously.					
I enjoy the good things of life and like to share them with my friends.					
I find it easy to change my mind and my actions when new facts emerge.					
When a group is suddenly without a leader I find myself taking charge of the situation.					
When important things are at stake I like time to plan, if that is possible.					
I have a keen sense of values and can spot a bargain anywhere.					
When I explain what I want done and why it is important, people generally do as I ask.					
I trust myself to act spontaneously.					

ful, creative, empathetic, a planner, and the like, that all weighs in your favor too—for trading or just for living.

You'll find that trading develops your potentials for living, just as living helps make you a more successful person at barter. But what if you find yourself sort of boxed in, with your personality just not geared to the give-and-take of exchanging?

There are specific things you can do about that, as you'll find outlined in Appendix 3. So don't worry about it now.

Just reflect that to have freedom, if you desire to use it, to operate anywhere on our exchange spectrum, is much like having a sharp knife and the opportunity to use it.

If careless, you *could* cut yourself with it. Yet that is not very likely if you exercise reasonable care.

If angered, you *might* hurt someone else with it. Still, if you are mature and congenial, there is little danger that you will do so.

It is more probable that you would find many ways to use such a tool for worthwhile projects you saw fit to devise.

So it is with a trader's ability to range anywhere on the operating keyboard. You are free to misuse this tool, just as if it were a knife. And some people do misuse their trading abilities. You need not do so, though, simply because you have the freedom to do so.

Loosen up your "can't" and "don't dare" and "mustn't" bindings so that you *may* if you choose, you *can* if you wish, and *dare to* if you see the risks as negligible.

Free yourself to entice, to offer symbolic or token payment, to use force if necessary, or merely to ask and to pay with a thank-you.

You may not choose to use some parts of this freedom, ever. But unless you have cut loose the ties that *prevent* your use of it, you limit your own power. You become aware of this lack of strength as you go about your daily process of living, with its exchanges at all levels. You find that, without inner power, you do not fare so well. Others have an unconscious (sometimes conscious) awareness of your limitations too.

It is in the interpersonal exchanges that our limitations show up first and strongest. If we are forced into lesser positions and worse deals every time we try to negotiate an exchange, due to our aptitude/ attitude lacks, we tend to avoid such situations.

Our chance of success in barter is then obviously limited. If we don't ever get into the competition, how can we expect to win?

If You Really Desire Success—Change!

It isn't difficult to locate any personality flaws you may have in trading.

One whole class of such limitations on free exchange we may call *compulsions.*

You can tick these off, in yourself or others. Someone you know is compulsively shy, for example. You can be sure that shyness will get in the way of profitable exchange at any level—social, educational, economic.

Or another person of your acquaintance is an inveterate buyer. Regardless of need, of value, or even of pocketbook, that person seems compelled to splurge on every shopping occasion. That person has real difficulty in trading, obviously.

Someone else is a compulsive talker. You would not trust him or her with any secret of yours; it would be blabbed to anyone available as a listener. You can imagine how such a trader would reveal all the warts and blemishes on merchandise he or she was offering to exchange. All that entirely apart from the fact that unending volubility annoys anyone who is trying to concentrate on other matters, such as a potential trade.

Still a different compulsive characteristic which will make trading difficult or impossible is fault finding or nitpicking. Such a habit will irritate or even outrage a trading partner so that no deal can ever be consummated. And that's even supposing the fault finder can ever locate merchandise, service or trader which meet his or her impossibly high standards.

Then consider the one who is compulsively suspicious. Without regard to persons, situations or other mitigating factors, an individual with this personality bias will find that the attitude drives away sound barter opportunities. (What honest trader will put up with continual doubt of his honesty?) Failing that, he will find it very difficult to overcome his suspicions sufficiently to carry out a trade.

Please continue to note and evaluate similar compulsive behavior traits in others as well as yourself. Keep seeing how they can and do interfere with exchanges of all kinds, as well as the simple trading we are most concerned with.

But then add to your list the habitual personality biases which have a typically emotional cast to them. Bear in mind that the presence of strong emotion limits the person's rational faculties, and constrains his general behavior to a level far below normal.

For instance, if a would-be trader is *afraid* of one-to-one interpersonal situations, you can be certain that this chap or gal will find it very hard to trade at a satisfactory level. (Fear tends to drive them away from the "danger" of a confrontation with some other person, so they find difficulty in staying put until an exchange has been worked out.) The other person in such an exchange has all the advantages.

The self-excusing *guilty* person likewise finds trading (or even social exchange) difficult to manage without getting the leavings as his or her portion. Guilt, low self-esteem, and the acceptance of the worse part as punishment for simply being, are seen together in the behavior of such *mea culpa* exponents. In trading, the guilty party seeks out the bad end of the deal. And generally manages to get it . . . even if it means seeing to it that no transaction at all takes place.

You probably know a few *touchy* people, requiring only the least word or perhaps hint of opposition for them to burst out in an angry tirade. Anger as a regular response to harmless remarks or situations strains normal trading harmonies to the breaking point. This is particularly true since angry people so often insist on being *right* (with the other fellow *wrong*, of course), whereas barter, like social interchange, is possible only when both parties and their values are relatively equal. Assuming that the angry person "wins" in the exchange, how often will an independent trading partner return for more of the same?

Someone full of *resentment* as an ongoing personal bias likewise runs into trouble in barter or any other exchange situation. The smoldering emotional level makes it very hard for the resentful person to carry on even conversational exchange. More protracted negotiations are even more difficult. And anyway, the resentful person's attitude sort of says "They're doing it to me and I can't stop them but I sure don't have to like it." What a trade-killer!

There are many more of these emotion-toned hang-ups you can spot in others or in yourself. (We all have them.) When you get to trading you'll notice them especially. They'll get in your way; you'll do well to get them out of your system.

Still another warp in the personality can come from an assessment, by the person himself, which limits his ability. This is every bit as defeating of attempts to act freely as the others we have mentioned.

A typical acceptance of this kind, although not related to barter in any direct way, is the perfect example because we have all heard it: "I could never be an artist—I can't draw a straight line!"

You have never seen a person holding such an opinion actually become an artist, either. And you very likely never will. Such a bias in the person's view of self makes it virtually impossible for him to take the time to develop whatever artistic talent he really does have.

The same situation, with a shift to other areas of experience, can and does occur with some who say they'd like to be traders. If anything of the kind shows up in your own observation of yourself, weed it out.

Typical biased assessments could be along these lines:

"I'd like to trade, but people always take advantage of me."

"You can't trust people."

"I'm no salesman—I couldn't sell a lifebelt to a drowning man."

"I'm just not creative enough to put deals together."

"How can I trade when I never can tell what something is worth?"

You can carry on from there. What you need to look for is any agreement you have with yourself which severely limits your abilities as a trader. The examples given may strike a responsive chord, or may not. No matter. Sum up your own views about yourself— as they would affect your trading—and do the little bit of work necessary to ease their hold on you. Having done so, you'll approach your barter experiences in a much better operating state than would otherwise be the case.

Whatever your position in life at the moment, your freedom to exchange and to exchange at better levels will be of benefit to you.

While the great majority of exchanging goes on without anyone's giving it much thought, and for meager stakes, a deft use of trading principles consciously applied can take you to the highest levels of power and influence.

In office politics, which you can observe in any organization or institution, there is a continual jockeying for power, position and the payoff in money and prestige. If you understand barter, and apply its principles to intangibles as well as tangibles, you can easily get ahead in the office power struggle. That's assuming you have freed yourself of your restrictive, self-imposed biases.

At higher levels of barter, while things and services change hands, the main element being traded is *power and influence*.

When congressmen or senators trade, that's what is at work: their influence or power to get things enacted, acted upon, or withheld.

In the higher spheres of commerce, education, the church, or anywhere else, such trading is what gets the work accomplished.

If you aspire to a place of power and plenty, you must then contrive to make your influence mean something. This comes as a result of eliminating from your personality any constraints that would limit your growth only to lower levels.

Add to this your personal desire, drive, intelligent application, and hard work, and you can carve out your own success to suit yourself. The desire, by itself, is not enough. All the other elements are necessary as well. It's up to you!

Once Again, Maestro, Please

- We're all involved in exchanging, on many levels, our whole lives through.
- Our own attitudes help determine whether we come out better or worse in these exchanges.
- Money—and one-for-one exchange— is only part of the whole exchange spectrum.
- Force, token payments, fraud, enticement, symbolic values, and many other means may be used to carry out exchanges.
- Simply asking for what you want can be the most effective way of getting it.
- Good traders are free to plan, persuade, act, and wait as necessary along all the points on the exchange spectrum.
- Good traders expect their offers to work out profitably, but if not, they are flexible enough to devise something else.
- If you check over your trading attitudes and aptitudes and find they could be improved, Appendix 3 gives a generally effective means for getting them adjusted to an easier level.

- The same method can also be utilized to alter habitual, narrow views of your capabilities ... to readjust repetitive emotion-toned responses ... and to smooth out overall restrictive views of yourself.

.. and ye shall eat the fat of the land.
—*Genesis* 45:18

CHAPTER 2

Ready ... Get Set ... Barter!

HAVING SET ABOUT BEING AWARE OF—and perhaps truing up—
any biases of yours which might interfere with profitable trading,
it's time to take stock of your situation at another level.

Just how are you fixed for bartering?

The most important consideration at the outset is that you *already* have a steady source of livelihood in cash before you begin
to trade. (If this is not the case with you, then before doing any
other sort of trading, negotiate a cash deal for your services so that
at least you have income enough for the necessities.)

I'll assume that you already have a job, perhaps a good one. Or
that you have a professional practice, or run a business, or have a
family member with such a setup to provide living requirements.
Attempting to make a full living from trading, especially at the
start, is asking too much of the world and yourself. It is better to
learn as you go, starting small, in your own environment. There
will be plenty of time later to decide whether you'd be appropri-
ately equipped to spend your full time in barter, or whether you'd
even care to.

Meanwhile ...

Barter Begins Where You Are

No matter how menial your job may be, how meager your skill, there is sure to be something you have to offer in personal skills which has a market value in the world of barter. (You are already trading that set of skills and knowledge for cash, aren't you?)

No matter how lofty your professional status or executive position, you can, *if you choose*, find the time or the items to trade for things or services. These may be things money can't buy, or which your tax bracket makes scarcely affordable in terms of money.

From the bottom rung of the economic ladder to the top, there are valid reasons for being active in barter. The reasons stem from the difficulties piling up these days for those persons stuck only in the money system.

If you find money hard to get, because you are in a low-end occupation or are just starting out in business life, you will find it is far easier to get things or services by trading than it is to struggle to find the cash to pay for them.

If you are in the comfortable middle brackets, adding cash to your income could move you into another bracket. But if you barter for a good many of the deductible business expenses you now pay cash to obtain, and save the cash, you are obviously money ahead. (We'll say it for the first of many times: consult your tax man about such matters to be sure where you stand individually.)

If you are in very high tax brackets already, trading may be the only reasonable outlet for your business skills. Money has become too costly for you to traffic in.

Or suppose that you are not even in the business world—you are retired, a mother stuck at home, a civil servant, or whatever. You no doubt really need extra income, but getting it as cash may be difficult or even against the rules of your job or pension. Barter may be exactly the solution you seek. By trading, you will find it easy to get into a little business of your own, giving you certain obvious tax benefits. And through it you can obtain some of the things otherwise too costly for you.

Where you are, only *you* know. What you want to get through barter, also, you alone can tell. But it will pay you to size up your situation realistically, rationally, so that you do not move ahead buoyed up by an emotional high and spurred forward by thoughts of easy gain. Trading and barter are relatively easy paths to follow to many of the good things of life. However, to utilize them effectively, you must put yourself on a practical base. That done,

Start Trading with What You Have

Make up an inventory, in written form, of what your trade goods or services are to be. That list may consist of nearly anything that might be sold for cash. Here are a few open categories:

• Professional services, or skilled services of all kinds.
• Regular merchandise or remainder merchandise or odd-lot goods.
• Handicrafts, objets d'art, and antiques
• Admissions, accommodations, transportation
• Real estate purchase or rental
• Advertising or publicity services

Pick something from this list, or create your own specialty. Determine exactly what you intend to offer in barter.

Whatever the commodity or service may be, make certain that in offering it you will not be upsetting your regular cash income.

Don't let barter take *merchandise* you need for your cash business. Don't set up your trading so it siphons off *time or services* required to keep your cash income flowing. *Don't let your bartering put you in bad with the tax authorities* (consult your tax man). And do not start to barter with anyone you are now selling *for cash*. Make sure your trade business supplements your cash business, that it becomes a definite *plus*, and is not a substitute for cash. (There may be exceptions to this rule in extremely high tax positions. See your accountant or tax lawyer.)

Perhaps a few thumbnail case histories of traders I have known, who started small and grew larger through barter, may help you see how you might begin. You'll find they involve services, merchandise, and professional expertise.

Six Case Histories of Barter Successes Who Started Small

Dal Nichols when I first met him operated a twenty-foot-wide restaurant in an old storefront building. It was located in the downtown section of a small city. There were many vacant shops on the same block, since most of the prosperous merchants had moved out to the malls when they were put up several years before. There was little foot trade. Cheap rent was the only apparent advantage of the location.

Dal was shrewd, though. He began to trade meals at his restaurant for many of the things he would otherwise have to buy for cash. He told me some of the things he obtained in this way: accounting services, printing, local newspaper ads, artwork for his menus.

Dal's business picked up rapidly, because of his good business sense and promotional ability. He obtained a long lease on the store next door—at a deflated per-foot price—and enlarged his restaurant. He bartered meals for much of the work of conversion, such as electrical, carpentry and carpet installation.

Next Dal worked out a part-cash, part-trade deal with the management of a major radio station whose offices and transmitter were nearby. Soon his commercials were drawing listeners from as far as fifty miles away. (In addition to the commercial messages, the station's air personalities chatted about Dal and his restaurant; Dal picked up the tab for their meals from time to time.)

The place was busy lunchtime, dinner hours, for supper, seven days a week. Dal issued his own house scrip. Then he seized an opportunity and bought a second restaurant, in a prime location but run into debt.

Dal assumed the existing debt structure and thus took over the operation with little or no cash outlay to the previous owner. He then settled practically all the small bills (those up to $250 or so) with restaurant scrip. For the larger accounts he obtained extended payments where possible and took care of them out of current cash flow.

Throughout, he was careful not to become overburdened with trade business, but mixed it judiciously into his rapidly increasing cash intake.

When I first met Dr. Larry Branstatter he had just opened a new optometric office. Then in his late thirties, he had, before going to school for his professional training, spent some time as a salesman. He used that experience in trading his way to a successful practice.

Among his group of friends were a lawyer and an advertising executive. Dr. Larry worked out trade-out deals with them and as a result soon found himself the head of a newly incorporated eye-research foundation (that was the lawyer's doing). Shortly thereafter, the ad executive began arranging radio, TV, newspaper, and magazine interviews through his public relations connections. Dr. Larry, as spokesman for his foundation, could present himself in ways which (he said) would not be ethical for an individual practitioner.

Dr. Larry's sales ability made it possible for him to present his interests so that he benefitted greatly from the reflected light.

With this as his main publicity and advertising thrust, he then used trade techniques wherever feasible. His markups gave him excellent leverage, so that he was trading profitably at all times.

The umbrella coverage of traded-for publicity and advertising quickly made Dr. Larry a well known professional in his part of the state. More important, perhaps, was the fact that they built his cash practice into a substantial success along with his reputation.

His trading activities continued. While still using barter to cover many business essentials, he found before long that he could also afford to trade for personal luxuries. Restaurants, resort accommodations, even travel, came his way through his barter contacts.

Dr. Larry told me, quite seriously, that he owed his success to his ability and willingness to trade for things other than cash.

Stuart McGregor is a successful entrepreneur in the carpet business. He is a producer of area rugs—those small decorative bits of carpeting used to enhance portions of rooms.

When I first knew him he was a salesman for one of the country's leading carpet mills, covering an area of a major city and selling to fine shops and certain key interior decorators.

Stu got into trading when his wife wanted to redo a portion of their home, and sought professional advice. Stu was too wise to pay for the whole decorator treatment, but selected an interior designer he trusted and offered to trade area rugs for decorating advice. (Mrs. McGregor then took the sketches and recommendations and did her own shopping.)

Stu bought "rems" (remnants) from his mill's cut-order department and had them bound, fringed, or otherwise finished to the decorator's satisfaction.

Stu bought the rems at about $1.50 a yard, he told me. But he indicated that as a finished area rug of perhaps three or four square yards it would sell at retail for at least ten times that much. Stu bought his decorator's advice at ten to fifteen cents on the dollar. (The decorator in turn worked the rugs into his jobs and billed them to his clients at top dollar.)

From this first whiff of success, Stu went on to exploit his trading advantage. He bought rems by the truckload, processed them through trade connections he knew, traded some and sold most for cash.

The little sideline quickly became the principal activity of Stu's working life. He resigned his mill connection, soon hired other salesmen, and was on his way to financial success.

I talked with him not long ago. Although selling mainly for cash, he does not miss a bet on trading. He had just arranged to have all his full-color brochures for the forthcoming selling season printed—in exchange for carpeting the offices of the printing company's new plant.

Jean Dangerfield is a fortyish lady I know in a sunny southwestern city. She paints, and paints very well. Some years ago, when she was just getting her pictures into one or two local galleries, she accidentally stumbled onto trading.

Her dentist was filling her teeth, and making small talk. When he found out that she was a recognized painter, he broached the idea of accepting a painting of his choice as payment for the work in hand.

From that early beginning, Jean traded at every opportunity. As her reputation in the galleries grew, it became easier to trade at satisfactory levels. She traded for home furnishings, for car leases, for beauty care, and even veterinary services for her pets. Not least of her trade arrangements was with a friend who was a publicist. That gave her much quicker fame throughout her entire region than her mere exposure in galleries could have done.

Although Jean's husband is a professional man, and their income more than adequate from his earnings alone, Jean's trading has added to it in important ways. Since she sells her work, she is thus in business. She is entitled to tax deductions for business-related expenditures. Many of her trade acquisitions offset sizeable chunks of cash, which then become available for investment or other purposes.

As Jean related it to me, it is amazing what can come out of a simple beginning, almost by chance. She now considers herself to be, and is, an extremely competent barter specialist. And a fine painter.

Pete Jender ran a flower-and-gift shop located in a major hotel. He had a substantial business on a cash basis, but hit upon trading as a way of extending the reach of his dollars.

Florists deal largely in perishables. Their markups are necessarily high to begin with. Pete routinely bought items at 15 to 20 percent of their retail price. When hand work and decorative materials went into the finished arrangement, as they frequently did, practical Pete marked up the items accordingly to even higher ratios.

This gave Pete considerable leverage. Items which cost him ten to fifteen cents could bring one dollar or more in cash—or in trade.

Pete started trading small, right in his own hotel.

He approached all the regular luncheon and dinner groups who had regular weekly or monthly meetings scheduled in the hotel. He offered to provide a floral arrangement for each of their meetings, to be offered as a door prize. All he asked was a brief announcement along with the award, stating that the flowers were courtesy of Pete's shop, Regency Flowers and Gifts.

That was relatively inexpensive advertising, and increased Pete's business considerably as time went by. Executives who were members of the various organizations to whom Pete gave the flowers thought of him first for their personal and business needs.

But the eventual masterstroke of Pete's trading genius came when he sent letters of credit worth $5,000 each to the several radio stations in his area. An accompanying letter simply stated that the station was free to draw on the credit at any rate it wished, for gifts to clients, as birthday or anniversary occasions required, for Christmas remembrances, and so forth.

Pete stated that he wanted to run a regular schedule of spots on the station, the year around, to be fitted into time slots the station had not otherwise sold.

There was no reluctance on the part of the stations. Such gifts are part of their everyday requirement. They saved the cash they would otherwise lay out for them.

You can see that Pete gained all-important advertising for his business at perhaps ten cents on the dollar. The station gained even more: its time is even more perishable than flowers, and it converted unsold time to the equivalent of cash.

Pete prospered. It wasn't too long before I heard of his latest venture: he was an active partner in a major real estate development in one of his city's better suburban neighborhoods.

Jim Yeats has a tiny jewelry store in a suburban neighborhood. It has little foot traffic. Jim opened his business there some years ago, after leaving the employ of a large jewelry chain-store group.

Despite the fact that he is in an out-of-the-way location, Jim has many things going for him. He is a jeweler, in the precious-metals-and-gems sense of the word. He is also an horologist. He repairs watches, but more important, he repairs clocks. One of Jim's first acts in business was to trade some of his jewelry stock to a nearby printer. In exchange Jim received business cards and other literature. One piece was a notice which Jim sent to all the other jewelry stores for miles around, offering to become their local clock-repair source at wholesale rates. The stores sent him an increasing flow of cash business for repair jobs which they re-billed at retail rates to their customers. Jim used these repair projects as a backlog, to keep him busy during lulls in his other work.

Jim managed to barter for most of the other things needed in his business. He set up long-term trading relationships. He was the first trader I ever observed personally who kept no dollars-and-cents record of his trade balances with others, or theirs with him. When he needed janitorial service, or printing, or his car fixed, he had a source ready to take care of it for him with no cash required. His fellow traders in their turn came to Jim when they needed an old watch repaired, or desired a new one, or wanted a birthday or anniversary gift. Jim has only one rule: "If you need it, you can have it. But if you want it just because you're greedy or intend to hoard it, forget it."

Jim keeps his business small; he prefers it that way. Yet his operation pays all his cash expenses, with investment capital left over. That is largely because he trades for so many things it frees up his cash.

What can we pick up from these stories, important enough to put to use in our own trading? These things, certainly:

- No matter what kind of business they were in, all these traders had a cash-producing activity to start.
- All of them began trading as an extra activity, right where they were, using their stock in trade as their trading capital.
- All used their creative imagination to make the barter activity pay off either directly or indirectly in cash business.
- They all were bold and direct in using barter techniques.
- Trading services or merchandise for advertising or publicity was almost standard operating procedure.
- Most were able before long to expand their businesses or branch out into other kinds of investment opportunities.

In your situation, the *details* are sure to be different. Just make sure you adhere to the same *principles*. You will thereby further your chances for success.

Which of These Big-Demand Items
Can You Provide?

While virtually any item of merchandise or kind of service can be sold or traded successfully, some goods and services are in much greater demand by traders than others.[1]

This appears to reflect both their high cash cost and their widespread need or desirability, in varying combinations.

Real Estate is the highest-priced commodity we are likely to buy. If you can supply real estate of any kind, you can move it readily if you are willing to mix barter with cash. (It moves even faster if you care to make it entirely a barter deal.) You can also barter real estate commissions, finders' fees, rentals, mortgages and trust deeds, and options. Barter accepted as part of a down payment, or as "boot," is an easy way to get active in real estate trading. Both high cash figures and the need for housing (or the desire to invest in land) make it a snap to get top value in return for real estate when trading.

Big-Ticket Consumer Goods are also easy to trade. If you can supply automobiles (new or used, for sale or lease) you can trade for many other commodities and services almost at will. The same is true and to just about the same degree if you can offer appliances, stereos, TV sets, furniture, home furnishings, or other consumer "capital goods" items.

High-Priced Specialty Services are generally just as easy to trade out as real estate and consumer durable goods. Doctors, dentists, lawyers, and accountants can, if they choose, trade out any portion of their fees with selected individuals who can supply what they wish. But you do not have to be a professional practitioner to do the same, trading at your top going rate. If you are a skilled craftsman, repair technician, bookkeeper, or stenographer, you can easily set up barter deals which will supplement your

[1] For a detailed analysis of 2,500 actual trading transactions, see Chapter 3.

cash income and actually net you more per hour than you would usually be able to obtain if you demanded cash for your services.

Consumer Goods of all kinds make fine trade stock. Everything from wearing apparel to food and beverage items to giftwares and small appliances are readily tradeable at full retail rates. Merchandise of good quality in new condition is better for trading than things in less saleable shape.

Consumer Luxuries such as furs and jewelry, watches and luggage, likewise are quickly snapped up when offered in barter.

Consumer Services of every description are especially good for trading. Everything from beauty care to babysitting, from auto repair to massage, can be bartered at full rates with little trouble.

Restaurant and Bar Service, hotel and motel accommodations, air travel, resort and cruise packages are highly prized barter commodities. (Some of the nation's largest barter companies specialize in just these kinds of offerings.)

Advertising in all its forms can be traded for virtually anything, as can its sibling, publicity. Hundreds of millions of dollars' worth of space and time is bartered every year.

Even Your Good Name or credit rating can be traded. Often the "front" for a new venture receives shares for lending his name and reputation; often someone in need of a loan will offer to pay or trade something of value to a cosigner on a note.

And Your Creative Work, of any kind, so long as it is of good enough quality to be worth having or using, can be traded for other things.

What it amounts to is that the question "What's tradeable?" can be answered by "What have you got to trade?" The items and services in largest demand for barter are precisely the commodities most popular for cash ... but if you can supply them, it's easier to *trade* than sell them.

How To Tip Values Your Way

Selecting things or services that are in demand is the first step in setting yourself up to start trading. The next step is to put your merchandise or services in presentable form, so their best features are emphasized and their apparent value upgraded.

If You Are Trading New Merchandise, make certain it looks new. Don't display it together with shopworn or broken cartons. If its original packaging is dirty or in disrepair, throw it away and just show the item inside. Be sure mechanical things are running properly. Include instruction booklets and guarantees, as well as all the necessary accessories, with the things you wish to trade. Attach the manufacturer's list price or prepriced sticker to verify its value in dollars. If none is at hand, then dig up an appropriate catalog to verify its worth.

If You Are Offering Used Goods, whether relatively new or antique, follow a similar procedure. Polish and shine, touch up, clean, tune and refurbish. If the thing needs repairing, and that is justified by the value you are placing on it, then repair it. This rule applies to anything you wish to trade, from an office building to an antique brooch.

If Your Trading Capital Is Services, then establish a "billing rate" for what you offer. Professional people such as lawyers and accountants will bill their time at so many dollars an hour. Doctors and dentists normally establish their rates for office visits and the various procedures, lab services, and appliances involved. If you are not a professional already using such a rate schedule, then set one up for yourself before you start bartering your services—even for cash. In doing so, there are two sets of factors to be kept in balance in order to arrive at an hourly rate (or per-item rate) for your services. First, the "going rate" for such services in your community. (You will want your trading rate to be positioned at the top of any such scale.) Second, your salary per hour multiplied by some number (usually from 3 to 5)[2] by which you arrive at a billing figure which will include salary, overhead, nonproductive time, and profit. In setting rates *never* set them anywhere near what you would receive on an hourly basis in a steady job. *Always* push your rates as near the five-times figure as local circumstances—and your own bravado—will allow. Whenever possible make *expenses* a separate cash consideration, not absorbed by you in your trade deal for services. Put your services together in a little list. Reproduce it by quick-print and make it part of your barter negotiations.

Showcasing is of Great Importance, whether you are bartering goods or services. Display merchandise in good, well-lighted surroundings. Antiques in a mansion sell at higher rates than when shown in a junk store; barter is just another kind of exchange. Park your auto for trade in front of a good hotel; meet a potential barter partner in a fine restaurant. Wear good clothes, drive a well-kept car (as new as you find expedient). All such devices are part of the systematic upgrading of values you will practice if you wish to make your trading activities really pay off for you. Make it a habit to think and do things on the "up" side of value rather than the reverse.

Ten No-No Barter Items

While it is a truism that you can trade *anything*, if you work hard enough at it and reduce your demands sufficiently, still there are some things which it is hardly worth anyone's time to fool with.

Entirely apart from *services* that are not of commercial or professional quality, and which quickly disqualify you if you offer

---

[2] Industry experience shows that it is necessary to mark up an employee's hourly wage by the 3 to 5 factor in order to cover overhead, lost/wasted time, bad debts, fringes, and profit. If one employs himself he'd best do likewise or else he'll never be a financial success.

them, some kinds of *things* are equally bad news for would-be traders.

Here are the eleven worst. When I was the president of a trade club, staging trade fairs regularly, I saw to it that traders offering such merchandise were forbidden to exhibit or sell it. It would turn off other traders from the whole event if permitted to continue.

Avoid offering:

- **Used Clothing.**[3] If you must get rid of it, give it to a charity and get a receipt you can use as a tax-deductible donation. Or hold a garage sale and dispose of it that way.
- **Used Furnishings,** unless they are antiques, or are in virtually new condition. Severely worn tables, chairs, and case goods should either go into the charity pile or else be refinished. Upholstered items should not have obvious worn, torn, or stained spots.
- **Used Cars** not in running condition . . . unless you are talking about an antique automobile, or are trading the old carcass as-is to a junkyard dealer or a youngster who intends to rebuild it.
- **Broken Equipment** of any kind. Either junk it or give it away. If it isn't worth your time and effort to get it in operating shape, why imagine it will be for someone else?
- **Bad Original Art, Ceramics, etc.** That means both esthetically and from the standpoint of workmanship. I am not talking about seconds of good pieces of ceramics, say, but inept design, painting, craftsmanship. Be sure your things are saleable for cash. Then trading is easy.
- **Pseudo Antiques.** There may be a fine line between antiques

---

[3] There are exceptions. The same day I wrote the list of No-No barter items I bumped into the operator of a cleaning plant who some months ago opened a used-clothing store. Customers bring in good-but-worn articles of clothing, he cleans them and sells them in the store. If not sold (at their asking price) in sixty days the customers can have them back again by paying the cleaning bill.

and junk, but if you step very close to that line you become a pariah as a trading partner. Leave the bad stuff where it is if you want to succeed in working out trading deals.

- **Flea-market Merchandise** is hardly worth its trouble, even for cash. Why bother with it in trading, when you can do so much better with no more expenditure of time and energy?
- **Carnival Gewgaws.** Don't imagine you can fool sharp fellow traders with the plaster dolls, shoddy teddy bears or pillows, with tin watches or colored-glass birthday rings. They have already explored avenues similar to those you'd have to follow in order to dig up such items. Concentrate on legitimate goods instead.
- **Fictitious Discount Deals.** This includes all the varieties of come-on coupon, worth so much toward purchase of photos, insurance, cars, vacation trips, or anything else.
- **Items Generally Available Free.** I've actually found people here and there trying to trade booklets from the various government departments (free if you write for them), as well as review copies of books (so stamped). But it can be any kind of merchandise.
- **Things Personalized to Someone Else.** There's always the possibility you can get around that, of course. I have re-used notebook covers (picked up for a song in quantity) by applying self-adhesive mylar labels to hide the original imprint. But generally, don't try.

Let's Check the Instant Replay

- Before you start trading for anything else, make sure you have a livelihood going on a cash basis. Use barter to go from there.
- No matter whether you are at the bottom or top of the economic scale, trading can be a relatively easy path to life's good things.

- Make an inventory of your trading capital, whether that is goods, services or a combination.
- Don't let barter interfere with your regular cash income. Use trading to add to it instead.
- Use your creativity to plan trading opportunities.
- Carry out your barter concepts boldly.
- Many kinds of things and services are attractive barter offerings, but don't forget your own creative work, reputation, and credit standing, which also may be traded.
- Tip values your way by making sure your merchandise is in top shape and well displayed in attractive surroundings.
- Attach price tags to goods when you have them, or reference your things in catalogs to establish a retail value. Devise a price sheet for your services unless you already have professional schedules of charges.
- Mark up your *salaried* hourly rate by a factor of three to five to arrive at a *billing* rate for your services.
- Don't bother offering used clothing, broken machinery or junk furniture as trading goods. Cars that don't run, amateurish art, worthless antiques, and similar trashy merchandise make you a trading outcast if you try to barter them.

*Mercantile morality is really nothing but a refine-
ment of piratical morality.*   —*Nietzsche*

CHAPTER 3

Cut Your Barter Teeth in a
Trade Club

EVEN THE MOST EXPERIENCED TRADERS I KNOW are members of
trade clubs (some even own them). There are advantages to the
most professional in belonging to a trading organization with
scores, perhaps hundreds or thousands, of other members, all of
whom are admittedly open to barter.

Beginning traders will find that membership in a trade club
may be their easiest introduction into the trading fraternity. Certainly it is an easier route than attempting to locate all those fellow traders out there with whom you'd love to trade, but don't
know how to reach.

Trade clubs offer advantages and opportunities, but they also
can become traps for the unwary. That's why this chapter is doubly important for you to study at the outset of your barter career.
When you join a trade club you agree to play a strange game by a
stranger's rules. You'll be wise to understand what goes on *in general* in trade clubs, so you can notice and be guided by warning
signs (or enticing invitations) emanating from the club or clubs
that interest you most.

Here We Go—into a Private Money System

Yes, in a trade club you haven't escaped into a world of pure barter. You are partway there, inasmuch as the importance of standard monetary units in the exchange process is minimized. Still, members think and act in terms of dollar valuations, even if dollars as such don't actually change hands.

Most trade clubs, like most other organizations, didn't just happen to form. True, there had to be a core of values (enticements?) in the idea of an organization devoted to trading, or else there would be no members. These values, while present, are present for about the same reason hay and oats are present for a horse: the owner has to provide something in order to get work out of the horse.

So trade clubs are organized by *someone* for that someone's advantage. Values to the members are present in just enough amount so that it is possible to get and maintain a sizeable number of traders within the organization. You can be sure, though, that few trade club owners give away any more than they have to in order to get what they want, just as the farmer doesn't overfeed his horses.

A trade club is governed by rules and regulations, important among which is the one which gives management the right to keep books on all transactions between members, and to charge a fee for each trade.

The creator of a trade club, the same as the organizer of any other kind of group, is free to draw up the rules to favor himself. That is also the case with the organizers of religions, governments, businesses, unions—you name it. My lawyer, Richard Sanders (a trader, of course!), puts it this way: If you are writing the contract, of course you'll write it the way you want it.

Such is the case with trade-club organizers. They write the contract, make the rules, enforce adherence to them. They do all this so as to benefit themselves. They include only such member benefits (or assumed benefits) as seem necessary to keep the club operating at a good level of trading. Essentially, club organizers set things up so as to be *in control.*

The first thing they control is the club's own accounting system, its ledgers of credits and debits following all the exchanges of each individual member.

The club may or may not print up forms that look like checks, or issue a plastic credit card or identification card. Still it will have some method established whereby members may validate their credit standing in order to obtain what they wish from other members.

The club may refer to its own debit-credit tokens as trade dollars, or as trade credits or units, as scrip, stamps, or by some other term. No matter what name is given, the units represent a private money system. The values nominally represented in the units are usually redeemable for things or services only within the individual club's own system. (There are exceptions, as we'll explain later.) The units are virtually *never* redeemable for cash at anything like their nominal valuation.

In order to keep its own business solvent, the club management, like the members, must have a mix of income which includes both cash and trade credits. It earns the cash by charging membership fees to those joining, and in some cases, annual membership fees in cash. The club also usually charges a cash fee on purchases. In addition, it charges a fee on its own credits on sales, collected when deposits are made. At least one large group of interrelated clubs charges a sizeable annual fee in cash and collects its transaction fees in trade units on each purchase.

The beginner in trade-club activities must learn not to think of club credits as dollar equivalents. Instead, it is better to think of them as a foreign currency, from a country ruled by a dictator, which can be spent only within that country and for things which the dictator permits and the citizenry are willing to relinquish in exchange for the currency tokens.

A friend of mine, Edward Auer (that's his real name), is a concert pianist with a tremendous popularity in Poland because of his brilliance in the Chopin repertoire. On his periodic tours there he is paid in Polish *zlotys*. Edward generally extends his tour to include a little vacation and shopping time when there, because he cannot take *zlotys* out of Poland. He can spend them only within that country's borders. That's the way it is with trade club chits.

So open your eyes in regard to trade-club value units. Be aware well before you join that:

- Trade dollars equate with U.S. dollars only nominally.
- You can generally spend them only within that club's system.
- They are usually discounted as you get them by the club's deposit-fee policy.
- Their value is likely to be discounted still further because you may have to pay a fee—cash or trade credits—when you spend them.
- You have to take the trouble to locate someone within the club who has something you want, and who will let you have it in exchange for the club's credits.
- You also must do all this while obeying the rules of the club well enough so that management doesn't freeze your credits so you can't trade them at all. (This happens when, for instance, you fail to pay your annual dues, or get behind in cash payment of transaction fees, or for other infractions of the owner-dictated club rules.)

There are other negative potentials in the private-money system of a trade club, as well as in any government's currency. We'll explore the major one—inflation—in a later section of this chapter.

Despite these hazards, there are very real values in utilizing trade-club currency in place of cash as far as you are able. For example:

- Most trade club members are pretty willing to spend their credits for what you have—your selling costs are cut practically to nil.
- You can get list price for goods with little quibble. No heavy discounting is necessary to work out trade-club deals.
- If you can take trade credits in at your top price, and then negotiate to spend them with other members at a fair price, you thereby release for other things the cash you have saved by the deal.

It may sound just a bit complicated. Actually it is simple.

Just reverse your thinking about trade dollars, as compared with regular cash dollars. Cash dollars are pretty hard to get, but very easy to spend. Trade dollars are quite easy to get, but may be difficult to spend.

Just be sure that you don't discount your own prices when you sell for trade dollars. Be certain that you don't waste your trade credits when you spend them (either for frivolous things, or through overpricing). Keeping those principles in mind, while acting as a prudent business executive would in the general trading situation, should see you doing very well in a trade club's closed credit system.

Hurray—Every Member's Already a Trader!

As the story goes, I've got good news and bad news.

The good news is that by simply opening your trade club's directory (if it has an "open" membership policy) you can locate members in many kinds of businesses and professions who are all there ready to trade with you.

The bad news is that, just as in any other population, there is a distribution which runs from the hyperactive on one end to the hypoactive on the other. In other words, from "good" to "bad" or from "always willing to trade" to "seldom or never get around to it."

This means that you must cull the membership in order to find active traders, and among those, work out deals for what you want.

Some more bad news: In every group there are a few members who are less ethical than the others, who drive sharper deals, who may even rip off the unwary. (It's no different in trade clubs than in the business world in general.) So you will need to identify and avoid these individuals. They are frequently well known to club managements, but are permitted to continue because they create fees by which the club lives.

Related to this is the fact that, as in any organization, some members of a trade club understand how to make it work for them and are very happy with the way things are. Most of the members in a going trade club at least make it work well enough to remain in the club. But there are a few in every club I have ever observed who are malcontents. These seem to fall into two classes, and you should avoid continuing contact with either once you locate them in any trade group you may join.

The first class, and usually a minor one, consists of those who joined but who have had little or no trade from other members. This may be due to their line of business, their location, or simply because the individual in charge of the business didn't know how to exert the minimal pressure required to bring all the trade business he could handle, or didn't care to. The relatively mild complaint of members of this discontented element is: "The club is no good—I've been a member for all these months and not one member ever bought anything from me."

The other class of malcontent can, and often does, cause great harm to an otherwise smooth-running trade club. These are the ones who have popular services or highly prized goods, and who let a lot of these go to their fellow club members. Then they just sit on their fat credit balances and moan. Their complaint, of course, is that while they opened their whole bag of goodies for the rest to pick from, they can't find anything when they themselves try to spend their credits. "It's all the club's fault."

Steer clear of these wailers, for your own psychological good. Believe me, no matter how overloaded members in a club may be, a good trader can still spend credits. He'll even bring in a new member, if necessary, in order to do so. And the simplest of promotional techniques is usually sufficient to stimulate a flow of credits for a member who really wants them. What's simpler than running a notice in the club's newsletter, bulletin or directory? Or asking to have a flyer touting your services enclosed with the club's monthly statement mailing? That is about all it takes.

If you listen too much to the unhappy few, you will begin to take on their attitudes. Don't do it. Single out the best traders you can pinpoint in the membership. Do business with them, ask their advice, adopt their attitudes and methods. You will prosper.

The idea that in a trade club everybody is already a trader needs to be modified, then.

Everyone in a trade club is *nominally* a trader. Among the membership, though, is a small group that understands so little about trading or barter clubs that its members neither appreciate nor deserve the advantages of a trade club. Another small group is composed of individual traders quite adept at exchanging and happy about the club and its positive features. These members appreciate the club, but would do quite well without it.

The bulk of the membership looms somewhere between these two extremes. You are free to orient yourself more toward one end or the other; but I would recommend that you aim for the happier end.

The Rules—the Club's and Yours

When you join a barter group you will be required to sign an application. Invariably, the rules and regulations are physically part of the application form itself, or are expressly incorporated in it by reference.[1] And in just about 100 percent of the cases, these rules require members to do these things:

- When members trade with one another, they must use the club's credit system to transfer values. In other words, no direct apples-for-oranges trading outside the system. Briefly, members are expressly forbidden to trade with each other *except* by use of the trade club's forms and procedures. This proviso is included in the rules and regulations by the club operator in the hopes that it will increase his "take" from transaction fees, which direct trading *without* using trade club procedures does away with. This in no way prevents a club member from direct trading with anyone who is a *non-member*.

- Deposits must be made within a brief period after every exchange between members. (The usual grace period is one week.)

- No handing-on of undeposited credits to third parties is permitted. (Doing so eliminates the club's transaction fees for the intermediate possessor of the credits.)

- A member cannot refuse to sell to another member unless he has already reached his trading limit (usually some multiple of one thousand credits) and has formally notified the club office in writing that he is now "on hold"—that is, temporarily not trading.

[1] A legal term. The application is usually only a single sheet; the rules and regulations often run to many pages. To make the rules and regulations binding upon the signer of the application, there is usually included a line such as " . . . and Applicant further agrees to abide by all rules and regulations of said Association, as they may from time to time be revised or amended, and said rules and regulations are hereby made part of this agreement as if they were physically incorporated in it . . .".

- A member must sell at his regular or (sometimes also) advertised price. (Kiting prices for trade purposes not permitted.)
- A member must pay all dues and assessments, transaction fees or other contractually spelled-out levies when billed. (Otherwise he may find his credit account frozen.)
- A member must sit still for unilateral changes in the rules or procedures, which may be promulgated from time to time at the option of the club management.

This is quite a formidable and restrictive array of *must-do's*. Only the promise of lucrative trading for the prospective member would induce him to try to do business under such restraints. Yet thousands of trade club members are apparently doing very well under just such rules. How can that be?

Active, aggressive traders can follow all the regulations of a typical trade club and do all right because their own profit spread on each transaction is sufficient to cover the fees involved and still leave a substantial net gain for themselves. (It's just like living with taxes.)

If you are careful to set up your own trading along these lines, you can adhere to the club's rules and do very well also.

Other traders do even better by *breaking* the club's rules—at least until they are caught.

These fellows avoid all fees if possible. They retain the credits they receive from sales and pass them along to other traders without depositing them. They use their club's directory as a source for locating others with whom they can set up direct trades, avoiding use of the club's credits entirely.

Some jack up their own prices when vending to another trade club member, thus artificially boosting their profit margin. Some, who may have arranged a windfall profit with little given in return, offer to pay more in credits than they would in cash in order to obtain hard-to-get merchandise. This starts an inflationary process that can quickly spread to include the whole membership.

Some wheeler-dealer traders belong to several trade clubs; others may belong to none. Yet in some parts of the country constant trading in various clubs' credits takes place, like an informal stock market, with values of one currency versus another fluctuating from day to day. But this activity reflects the relative instability of the respective clubs' trade units and does not involve large amounts of credits from the more conservatively managed organizations.

As a beginning trade-club member you are free to plot your course as you choose. I would recommend, though, that you stick pretty close to the club's rules—as adapted to your circumstances in the light of what this book tells you.

Do not formulate your own trade-club philosophy until after you have read and studied chapter 8, 9, or 10 of this book (whichever applies to your situation as a retailer, professional or craftsman).

Every Time You Trade You Get Nicked a Fee

Suppose you're a retailer, and sell to a fellow club member.

In general, your trade-club rules spell out that your deposit *automatically* goes into your account in their computer minus a fee. This may be as little as 2 or 3 percent, or as much as 10 or 15. Some trade groups have categories of businesses and professions; fees may vary for each category.

For the most part, the fees collected on deposits from sales are in *trade credits*. This is because trade dollars are "softer" and easier to collect than cash dollars. Club managements want deposits to be made, therefore they levy fees in *credits* on the seller. (Some clubs even skip this fee entirely, but charge a big annual cash membership assessment and levy the trade-credit fee against each buyer.)

Cash fees are generally collected from buyers. The theory is, a trade-club member with a bunch of credits to spend is willing to pay cash for the privilege of laying the credits off on a fellow trader. The theory seems to work pretty well in practice.

It will depend upon the particular trade-club setup just how the cash fees are collected.

Some collect the cash in advance, as annual dues.

Some collect the cash in advance, as a fee, before the trade markers (checks or scrip) are issued to the member, or credit is okayed.

Some clubs bill members for cash transactions, and generally have trouble collecting the fees.

At least one major club collects the fees by electronic funds transfer (or by bank draft) directly from members' bank accounts or bank charge accounts (VISA or Master Charge).

Don't think you can avoid payment of the club's charges for long. Either you'll be caught cheating and be thrown out of the group, or you'll be penalized by having your account sealed until you pay up.

The best policy is to know these facts of trade-club life, and to be prepared to live with them and to prosper in spite of them.

Ah—but Who Guards the Guardians?

Juvenal said it in his *Satires* nearly two thousand years ago: "But who would guard the guards themselves?" Lord Acton put it: "Power tends to corrupt; absolute power corrupts absolutely." The American founding fathers were aware of this problem of human nature, as the system of safeguards they built into the Constitution attests. State and federal governments have regulated field after field of human activity when the unregulated conduct of entrepreneurs has been shown to be obviously against the public interest. Thus we have strict licensing laws for doctors, dentists, barbers, and beauticians, for contractors, real estate and stock brokers, and franchisers. States charter banks and control their activities according to strict rules. But so far as I am aware, there has been no law enacted anywhere which sets up performance standards for trade clubs or barter associations, or which limits their activities as a private money system.

The law of the ancient marketplace prevails: *Let the buyer beware.*

The temptation is always present for trade-club operators to float an overabundant supply of their own credits. They use these to buy from members for their own account.

Obviously, in order to keep trading active and growing, there must be a reasonable supply of credits within the system. Otherwise, the existing supply of credits becomes locked up in members' reserves and there is little business done. The trade club operators *should be* living in part off their cash fees, and in part from their fees taken in club credits. However, they *may be* living partly off their own "float"—credits which they issue to themselves and spend as if they had normal value.

Well-run trade clubs do little or none of this. Instead, funds needed to generate additional trade volume are created in the form of loans to members—which are paid back out of sales they make to other members. This plan keeps debits and credits in balance. Management in such cases is conservative, as bank managements tend to be. Their credits are sound and readily acceptable among the members as alternatives to cash.

The overfloated currency of a poorly run club, though, will have little value. Members are reluctant to accept it. Trades, if they occur at all, are at multiples of the dollar price-tags involved, or are between old-timers in the club and wide-eyed newcomers who know no better.

Before you join any trade club, no matter how tempting its offer, check out its realities by talking with some of its members. Don't call or go see just those the club's sales rep or management suggests. They're likely to be hand-picked. Instead, ask to copy a dozen names at random out of their directory, or have them provide you with all their names beginning with P or F or L or some other letter.

Call or go talk with as many as you think you need to of these random-choice members. Ask them about their experience with the club. Here are some significant questions:

- How easy do you find it to spend your credits with other members?
- How willing are you to accept the club credits yourself? If I were to join, could I come over right away and lay off my first batch of credits with you?
- Do you find other members boosting their prices when you want to spend credits with them?
- Do members try to hustle you into selling to them by offering you more than standard prices?
- How do you rate club management with regard to general policies and administration?
- Do you find that management or sales reps are first on the scene to buy from new members who enter the club?

Questions such as these should tell you, within a few calls, all you need to know about a particular organization before you decide whether or not to join it. If the indicators show up pretty much on the dark side, be alerted by that fact. Don't be so simple as to believe you will be treated differently than are present members.

Just because I have been emphasizing some of the things to be wary about in trade clubs, don't for a moment think I am talking about all such groups as miscreants. That would be far off the mark. All of the large clubs I have information about are highly ethical and solvent. Their members, for the most part, are treated fairly and are glad to be part of their trading programs.

Indeed, you may be safer in signing up with a large national trade club than with one local to your area, although much of the fun of barter disappears when it is computerized and highly organized, as most activity in the large clubs is today.

My remarks are in no way an indictment of the trade-club field as a whole. They are rather based upon my observation of what *can* happen, as I have *seen* it happen, in trade clubs (now defunct or nearly so) of which I have been a member in times past.

How to Make Sure You're Priced for Profits

Since it costs you money to join a trade club, and cash fees while you're a member, you'd be well advised to plan to make a profit on your trade volume while you are a member.

Since we are dealing with percentages which probably average out at about 10 percent on transactions, you can easily see that your normal profit on merchandise or as a return on time and service is that much less than normal. If you are in a line of goods in which you find your retail by dividing your cost price by, let's say, 0.6 (40 percent discount), the 10 percent taken by the trade club is obviously 25 percent of your profit.

Shorter discounts and you're even worse off. To this profit loss you must also add the extra time and trouble *in general* it takes to set up and transact barter business when you want to spend your credits; your real profit is cut still further.

Obviously, then, straight trading for standard merchandise or services at normal markups will leave you in the hole as compared with cash sales. Some trade clubs have a provision permitting members to ask part cash in trading their stock of high-cost, cash-intensive merchandise. (One national trade club *requires* part payment in cash on all retail transactions.) This tends to ameliorate the situation somewhat. You will thus get back part of your inventory cost, and should pay fees only on the *trade-credit* portion of the transaction.

Even so, you can make this kind of arrangement really attractive only when you make it a matter of policy to establish long-term, large-volume trading relationships both to obtain and to spend trade dollars.

Professionals, artists and artisans, and service people have a better break. Really all they must do is trade time and skill for trade credits, with perhaps a small amount of material tossed in. Even so, if you are a professional in one of these areas, double-check your pricing before you become a member of a trade club. Make sure your scale of charges really permits profitable trading.

You can, if you choose, offer to barter only certain merchandise, or particular services. Merely insist on that provision in your agreement when you join the trade club. Just attend to it *before* committing yourself to a contract that could involve a great deal of unprofitable trading.

Watch Those Fees ... They Can Kill You!

While trade clubs must charge for their services in order to render their very worthwhile services to members, the steady drain of fees can seriously deplete profits unless you are alert to what goes on.

To make doubly sure you understand how the fees operate in trade-club transactions, let's take a typical example for analysis.

A trade club, as standard policy, charges 5 percent in trade credits on sales. It charges 8 percent on purchases in cash. (This is the actual percentage from one of the national trade organizations; the exact figures vary from club to club, however.)

Another member buys from you, let's say, 100 trade units worth of your goods or services. Here's what happens:

Sale of your stock in trade	100.00
Less 5 per cent seller's fee	5.00
Net deposit in trade units	95.00

When you spend those trade credits, whether in one chunk or in several chunks, you must pay another fee:

Purchase of goods or services	95.00
Cash buyer's fee @ 8 percent	7.60

The net effect is that it costs you $5.00 in trade credits and $7.60 in cash in order to obtain 95 net spendable trade dollars. We cannot convert cash and trade dollars into the same units for figuring percentages on the total, but if we could it would work out to paying a fee of a little more than 13 percent.

From this you can easily deduce that you'd better make certain that your contract requires you to pay transaction fees *only* on the trade portion of deals with other members which involve part cash. Otherwise your effective fees on trade dollars will be much higher.

Also, if you are buying or selling real estate, you might try to negotiate a better percentage on the fees than the one which is set for smaller transactions. We'll assume that you are paying fees only on the down payment or broker's commission, not on the entire purchase price. Even so, reducing the percentage can make a tremendous difference in your expenditures.

Here's a typical instance, based on the same 5 percent trade on the sale and 8 percent cash on the purchase:

You make a down payment in trade dollars	10,000.00
Your cash buyer's fee @ 8 per cent	$800.00

If you can negotiate even a 2 percent reduction in the rate charged, you will pay (at 6 percent) $200.00 less. The time to negotiate is *before* you join the club, if possible. If not, then try to get club management to reduce its fees for real estate deals before you get into any specific transaction which commits you to pay in trade dollars.

On the other face of such deals, as the seller receiving the trade credits, you will be required to deduct 500.00 credits from your deposit. Here again, if you can wangle a better deal you'll be credits ahead.

If you are actively engaged in real estate, by all means study Chapter 12 in detail.

Thumbnail Outline of Trade-Club Trading

In Chapter 2 I gave my general impressions of the kinds of things which are in demand among traders. At this point you may wish to examine in detail an analysis of 2,500 actual trade-club transactions. This is probably as close as you will ever get to knowing *exactly* what products and services are in demand, and in what proportions.

You might not puzzle out significant details from the listing itself, so I will provide them here:

Analysis of Percentages by Categories

Business Type	% of Sales	% of Volume
Restaurant	38.92	4.33
Dry Cleaner	3.16	0.51
Real Estate	1.32	34.99
Advertising	3.28	9.29
Printer	3.44	2.37
Dentist	2.52	3.06
Auto Service & Repair	3.68	2.12
Hairdresser	6.44	1.23
Jewelry	1.44	4.53
Landscaping & Gardening	0.76	4.35
Auto Accessories	2.80	1.76

These figures might change by season of the year, or other factors, but I'd say study the list carefully. It may give you a good idea what line or lines you might want to offer especially to traders.

Analysis of First 2,500 Transactions, August 1978

Business Type	Number of Transactions	Volume	"Trade Dollar" Average
Restaurant	973	12,543	12.89
Hairdresser	161	3,549	22.04
Auto Service & Repair	92	6,126	66.59
Printer	86	6,856	79.72
Advertising (publications)	82	26,880	327.80
Dry Cleaner	79	1,472	18.63
Auto Accessories	70	5,089	72.70
Clothier	66	2,714	41.12
Dentist	63	8,861	140.65
Chiropractor	48	2,957	61.60
Flower Shop	39	1,242	31.85
Jewelry	36	13,107	364.08
Optometrist	35	3,781	108.03
Hotels & Motels	35	2,206	63.03
Real Estate	33	101,256	3,068.36
Sporting Goods	32	4,052	126.63
Food Sales	32	575	17.97
Doctor	31	2,370	76.45
Office Machines & Supply	30	1,347	44.90
Equipment Rental	24	1,863	77.63
Building Construction & Repair	21	8,458	402.76
Art Sales & Supplies	20	3,905	195.25
Landscaping & Gardening	19	12,591	662.68
Lawyer	19	6,029	317.32
Graphics & Typesetting	16	3,296	206.00
Signmaker	16	2,480	155.00
TV Sales & Repair	16	1,134	70.88

Analysis of First 2,500 Transactions, August 1978 (Cont.)

Business Type	Number of Transactions	Volume	"Trade Dollar" Average
Car Wash	15	257	17.13
Building Materials	14	1,353	96.64
Pool Service	13	765	58.85
Car Lease & Rental	12	2,790	232.50
Photo Studio	12	1,067	88.92
Pet Supply	12	275	22.92
Animal Hospital	12	136	11.33
Answering Service	11	796	72.36
Interior Fixtures	11	2,534	230.36
Appliance Sales & Repair	11	2,168	197.09
Mailing/Distributing Service	11	1,801	163.73
Building Maintenance	11	1,708	155.27
Health & Swim Club	10	427	42.70
Drapery Cleaners	10	709	70.90
Carpet Sales	9	2,690	298.89
Solar Products	9	903	100.33
Carpet Cleaner	9	824	91.56
Household Items	9	639	71.00
Exterminator	9	366	40.67
Cinema Tickets	9	300	33.33
Beauty Supply	9	278	30.89
Bookstore	8	143	17.88
Moving & Storage	7	972	138.86
Plumber	7	277	39.57
Dog Groomer	7	128	18.29
Pharmacy	7	49	7.00
Accountant	6	1,825	305.17
Shoes	6	158	26.33
Films & Records	6	136	22.67

Analysis of First 2,500 Transactions, August 1978 (Cont.)

Business Type	Number of Trans- actions	Volume	"Trade Dollar" Average
Locksmith	6	99	16.50
Furniture Sales	5	3,020	604.00
Upholsterer	4	1,420	355.00
Psychologist	4	406	101.50
Computer Service	3	5,875	1,958.33
Security Systems	3	3,461	1,153.67
Drapery Sales	3	851	283.67
Coffee Service	3	237	79.00
Travel Agency	3	165	55.00
Music Lessons	3		37.67
Secretarial Service	3	69	23.00
Dental Lab	2	285	142.50
Catering Service	2	200	100.00
	2,500	289,414	115.77

This analysis is reproduced here through the courtesy of Mutual Credit, Los Angeles, and is used with its permission.

Trade-Club Trading Success
A Case History

Hank Gray is a publicist, and a good one. He runs a one-man operation, with a stable of clients ranging from industrial to institutional to professional. His first experience with a trade club began about ten years ago, when he became member '17 in a club just being formed.

Savvy in the ways of business—if not of trade clubs—Hank made it a condition of joining that he be given the publicity account for the trade club itself. This was arranged by the hungry club management, for a fat fee payable in trade credits.

Hank began arranging the usual interviews and stories for the club officers, tapping the credits bank for expenses as incurred. (Hank took editors to lunch at a restaurant which was also a trade-club member. In addition he picked up suitable gifts when he judged them necessary, using them to relax editors' uptights, all on club credits and outside his regular fees.)

He suggested that the club should have a company publication, to use both as a medium to keep the members aware of news events and as a recruiting tool to get new members. He arranged to get an extra budget for this.

These various activities kept Hank in close constant touch with management decisions. Often opportunities arose to take advantage of bargains, or once-only offers. He picked up an office copier and an electric typewriter for 100 percent trade credits—and outfitted himself with custom-made suits and Italian imported boots and shoes, also on trade. He arranged a convention at a resort hotel which joined the club, and picked up the tab in trade units, then collected in cash from his regular client on whose account he had set it up. (Hank was not troubled by the thought that such conduct might be considered unethical. Simply a way of cashing out on his trade dealings, was the way he saw it.)

Hank used the same tactics in obtaining printing for clients. He also arranged to have his accounting done by one of the club members, at 100 percent trade, and his answering service was also a trade-out.

When he required occasional heavy typing he had that done by a secretarial service—also a club member.

In short, since Hank was an entrepreneurial type to begin with, and was used to working out deals, trade-club credits opened up a new world of activity and profit.

He did not slough off any of his normal cash clients, but added to them the highly lucrative trade-club account. The easily earned trade dollars brought him some luxuries he would have been reluctant to buy for cash. More important than that, the trade credits replaced cash (or even turned into cash) so that his regular dollars went much farther than they ever had before.

Trade-club trading: "How I love it!" was how Hank phrased it to me when he related his experience with it.

Keep Your Eye on These Important Points

- A trade club may be an easy introduction to trading—but it also may have traps for the unwary.
- Trade clubs operate their own private money systems, and are organized for the profit of the owners with incidental benefits to the members.
- Club rules let management handle the books on all transactions between club members, and charge fees for the service it performs.
- Fees are collected both in trade dollars and in cash, though rules vary among clubs.
- Trade currency is usually redeemable only within its own club system, much like the blocked currency of a foreign nation.
- Trade dollars are worth their equivalent in U.S. currency only nominally. If you could sell them for cash they would bring only a fraction of their face value.
- Trade dollars are generally already discounted by the time they are credited to your account, and are further discounted by fees collected when you spend them.
- Sift through the membership of a trade club to find who the active traders are, and which ones you'll feel okay in trading with.
- Avoid the small minority of complainers you'll find in every trade club (or other group, for that matter).
- Study the club's rules and be prepared to work within them; but make any stipulations you judge prudent before you sign up.

- There's always the possibility that trade-club owners will float more trade dollars in the system than the membership's trading activity warrants. Check out a few members before you join to learn how tight a ship the management is running.
- Before you join a trade club, make sure that your profit structure is right for profits in trading for club credits.
- Negotiate any special dispensations you see you'll need *before* you execute a contract with a trade group.
- Restaurants account for a huge number of trade transactions, but only a fraction of the trading volume of a typical club. Real estate sales, however, while numbering only about 1.5 percent of transactions, account for more than one third of the total volume. Study the activity of the various categories of business and professions before deciding just what you should offer in a trade club.

Government is emphatically a machine: to the discontented a "taxing machine," to the contented a "machine for securing property." —*Thomas Carlyle*

CHAPTER 4

Start Off Right with a Trading CPA Accountant

YOU NEED A CPA ACCOUNTANT who is himself a trader, and for two good reasons.

The first and obvious one is that a good CPA can be an excellent pilot to help you chart a safe course through the rocks and shoals of tax laws. And second, if your CPA is a trader himself he'll better understand the peculiarities of accounting for barter transactions. There's also a further plus: If your CPA is used to trading, he'll no doubt trade with you so you'll be cash ahead.

In selecting the CPA you'll feel comfortable to have as your guide, you may want to check out a few before choosing the right one for you. The reason for this is pretty basic. You'll want to have a man careful and conservative enough to keep you clean with the tax people, yet with sufficient wheeler-dealer savvy not to let you pay any taxes you don't legally have to pay. And the advice you'll get can vary widely.

A Trade Dollar Is a Dollar—or Isn't it?

One CPA I talked with told me flat out that it is not only legally but morally obligatory to report every barter transaction as if it were cash. (He is an active member of a large trade club, too.)

He declined to be quoted by name—as most professionals in this field do—but the substance of this argument was this:

"We are legally required to pay income taxes. Barter counts as income; therefore we must figure such transactions into our tax accounting.

"Not only that, but morally we are obliged to consider it as income also. We live under a system of laws, based on our constitution. The great leaders who set up our government structure were carrying out God's command to bring forth a new order for mankind on this continent. We who live here and benefit from such laws are bound to respect them with regard to paying taxes levied under those laws."

That's a pretty extreme position, I think, but it is certainly adhered to by some accountants and perhaps many patriotic citizen-clients.

Just as extreme, but utterly different, is the advice of John Freeman, Seattle constitutional lawyer and tax attorney. John said to go ahead and quote him:

"Don't report any barter transaction. Forget the IRS. The income tax law is unconstitutional anyway, and in any due-process proceeding you'd go scot-free."

I'm sure that Lawyer Freeman has many clients who follow his advice; he has calls to appear on behalf of business people in many parts of the country. I even know a couple of traders who follow his advice.

For you to do so, though, would no doubt be pretty risky. Better find some more satisfying middle course between reporting nothing and accounting for everything you trade. Finding a realistic-minded CPA for your own counsel and strategy can help you do this.

The IRS: A Dollar Trade = A Dollar Cash

Elsewhere in this chapter you'll find excerpts from current IRS publications, treating various aspects of exchange and sales. This following material is excerpted from an IRS bulletin circulated to accountants in Southern California during the summer of 1977. In reading it, remember that Southern California is a hotbed of trade-club and independent barter activity:

> **Income and Profit from Bartering Goods and Services** should be computed in the same manner as though cash was involved. Profit from the sale or exchange of property or services—in the ordinary course of business—is specifically includible in income. If property constitutes an asset normally includible in inventory or sold during the normal course of business, then the character of such income is ordinary. Profit is generally easy to determine in barter situations, as the cost and retail price of goods are known, and may generally be used as a measure of the fair market value. Additionally, all income or gain (profit) should be determined at the time of sale; no deferment exists for subsequent completion or delivery, nor for the subsequent passing of title if all parties regard title as passing at the time of sale. In general, then, treatment of income and profit should be no different when goods or services are bartered than if such goods or services were sold for cash.

That makes it pretty clear what the IRS would like accountants to tell their clients about barter, in a time and place where it could have been causing problems in revenue collection.

More generally, though, the Internal Revenue Service takes a broader view of sales and exchanges. The citations which follow are taken from the 1979 edition of Publication 544 of the IRS, titled *Sales and Other Dispositions of Assets*.[1]

Sales. A sale is generally a transfer of property for money only or for a mortgage, note or other promise to pay money.

Exchanges. An exchange is a transfer of property in return for other property or services and may be taxed in the same way as a sale, see Nontaxable Exchanges . . .

Gains and Losses. A *gain* is the excess of the amount you realize from a sale or exchange over the adjusted basis of the property you transfer. A *loss* is the excess of the adjusted basis of the property over the amount you realize . . . The amount realized from the sale or exchange of property is the sum of any money received plus the *fair market value* of any property or services received . . . *Fair market value* is the price at which the property would change hands between a willing buyer and a willing seller, neither being under any compulsion to buy or sell, and both having reasonable knowledge of the relevant facts. Assignments of value to the property by parties with adverse interests in an arm's length transaction are strong evidence of fair market value. For notes or other evidences of indebtedness, which you receive as part of the sale price, the fair market value is usually the

---

[1] Other IRS publications you may find of interest in puzzling out your own trading strategy include #525, *Taxable Income and Nontaxable Income*; #534, *Tax Information on Depreciation*; #535, *Tax Information on Business Expenses and Operating Losses*; and #550, *Tax Information on Investment Income and Expenses*. The IRS has plenty more. Just telephone or drop in at your district director's office and explain what your interests are. They will mail the publications to you free. The publications are also sold by the Superintendent of Documents, U.S. Government Printing Office, Washington, D.C. 20402.

best amount you can get from the sale to (or discount with) a bank or other buyer of such paper . . .

Nontaxable Exchanges. Gain from certain exchanges of property is not taxed, nor is loss deductible, at the time of the exchange. The new property is treated as being substantially a continuation of the old unliquidated investment . . . Exchange of property for like property is the most common type of transaction in which no gain or loss is recognized. However, the following strict conditions must be met:

- *Must be business or investment property.* Both the property you trade and the property you receive must be held by you for business or investment purposes. Neither property may be used for personal purposes such as your home or family automobile.
- *Must not be property held for sale.* Neither the property you trade nor the property you receive may be property you sell to customers. It must be property held for productive use in your business and classified as a fixed asset, or property held for investment. Machinery, buildings, land, trucks, and rental houses are examples . . . The nontaxable exchange rule does not extend to inventories, raw materials, accounts receivable, or other current assets, nor for real estate held for sale to customers by dealers.
- *Must be like property.* The exchange of real estate for real estate and the exchange of personal property for personal property are exchanges of like property. For example, the trade of an apartment house for a store building or a machine for a truck, is a like-kind exchange . . . An exchange of personal property for real property does not qualify; for example, the exchange of a piece of machinery for a store building. The exchange of livestock of different sexes is not a like-kind exchange.
- *If you pay cash* in addition to the property you give up,

you still have no gain or loss if the previous conditions are met.

You must keep in mind that this is only a brief excerpt. Read the whole of Publication 544 and other IRS bulletins for a more complete picture of taxable and nontaxable exchanges, capital and noncapital assets, gain and loss, and so forth. Also please understand that this is not the law itself we are looking at, but a popularized summary of it. Hence it is not appropriate to draw firm and lasting conclusions from this material, although we can reasonably explore some aspects in a tentative manner.

Since you will no doubt find it convenient to use your trade club and its accounting system for much of your trading, and since there appears to be no ruling specifically applying to such systems of credits, let's pick up that angle first.

Dick Palmquist (that's his real name) operates a trade club out of his business headquarters in Pixley, California. That's a small town in the San Joaquin Valley north of Bakersfield.

Dick calls his credits "trade notes." They have a par of $1.00 and he even redeems a small quantity of them at par each month. A couple of years before this writing someone—still unidentified—asked the Securities and Exchange Commission the question: "What is a trade note?"

The SEC's San Francisco office demanded that Dick spread out all his records; Dick agreed to do so provided the proceeding was at an open meeting with the general public invited. And much more.

Since Dick Palmquist also publishes a newspaper and operates a radio station, and in general takes a very strong and assertive stand about his constitutional rights, the proceedings dwindled and died without anyone's ever having determined the key question: "What is a trade note?"

The SEC made no ruling about a "trade note" nor, to my knowledge, has it defined any other trade-dollar entity. The IRS does not mention trade credits of the kind issued by trade clubs in any of its literature I have examined, nor do the federal tax guides (Standard, Prentice-Hall, etc.) make reference to them.

An Accountant's View:
It's a Dollar Only When Spent

If they are not defined, how to handle them in accounting? That was the trade-credit question I asked a CPA in Los Angeles. Here in summary is the answer. (As usual, he said "Don't use my name.")

"Since trade credits or trade dollars are not defined, we may classify them as promissory notes of no established market value.

"A promise to pay by itself is not enough to call up the doctrine of constructive receipt. When the note has no established fair market value when received and cannot be converted into cash it does not represent income on a cash basis to the one who receives it.

"Also, if there is no established fair market value at the time of receipt it is not income to the accrual-basis recipient either, because the absence of a firm and definite value shows that it is doubtful whether it can be collected in full.

"However, as regards cash-basis taxpayers, such a note may be included as income if—and to the extent that—a fair market value can be determined."

This CPA amplified his statement by saying that in his view the value of a trade credit could be determined only when spent; and its fair market value as of that moment determined its dollar equivalent as income.

I am not an accountant, but it seems very clear to me that a shrewd CPA coaching a willing trader could work out some means of sheltering some trade income in this nebulous area of nondefinitions.

One Club's View: Dump the Transaction Records

It is one thing to attempt to reduce the value of trading dollars, for instance by not counting them as income until spent, or perhaps discounting them heavily before classifying them as income.

It is another thing entirely to let them vanish into an electron cloud of dispersed computer records so that it is as if they never existed.

What the various trade-club managements across the land are doing as a matter of general policy, I do not know. I do know that several years ago one major trade club announced to its membership that effective as of the date named it would henceforth routinely destroy its computer memories of transactions at the end of twelve months.

Ostensibly the move was to simplify the club's data-storage procedures. Twelve months is time enough, we'd agree, in which to iron out any accounting disputes between member and management or vice versa.

But then you might think, Just how much room does it take to store transaction data electronically these days? How many inches of shelf space does it take for a month's—or a year's—exchange records? Or if that couple of inches is too precious to waste, why not utilize microfiche?

It quickly becomes clear that there must be some other motive in clearing out the old sales information than lack of space or desire for tidiness.

The real reason, we suspect, is so that transactions will be hard to trace beginning at about the time a tax audit might plausibly be under way for some club member.

If this guess is correct, then a further assumption is justified: There must be widespread nonreporting of trade-note receipts as income among trade-club participants. The president of the trade club mentioned told me that while a couple of the group's members had been investigated on tax matters, the club itself had not.

Any demand to see the club's records by tax authorities would be referred to the group's attorneys, he said.

I'll assume that the next few years will bring forth increased interest in trade-club trading on the part of the Internal Revenue Service, and that after litigation and perhaps legislation there will emerge a set of definitions for income to include trade credits. Meanwhile, feel free to join the pioneer explorers of this *terra incognita* of the tax world.

What's the Safest Course for You?

The safest course—the path that's easiest—is to count all trade exchanges as the IRS demands: the same as cash. This is to take that well-worn pathway at the middle of the exchange spectrum we talked about in Chapter 1. This is safest; it is also the dullest. It may even be the least profitable course.

Only you can determine your optimum method of accounting for trade transactions; and only then after consulting your tax accountant or tax lawyer in detail.

Still, there is a lot of unknown territory out there to explore, and it could be exciting, challenging, and rewarding to see what's there for you.

If you can loosen up your habit patterns enough to do so, you might begin to think creatively in this area. I provide a few random thought-stimulator ideas just to get your own mental gears to mesh.

In order to shelter the maximum of your trading income— hence realize the most profit—what if you were to:

- Set up a special corporation to handle all your trading. This might be a nonprofit corporation, or a Subchapter S or other entity about which you and your CPA and lawyer can agree.
- Plan to trade only nonroutine items, which are not part of your general business inventory.

- Arrange to trade only for business-related things which would be normally deductible anyway, thus freeing extra dollars which you can utilize any way you choose.
- Consider donations in trade goods or trade scrip to a charitable organization qualified under the IRS rulings. If your bracket is right, this could have the effect of taking the place of a cash donation, reducing your net income thereby.

These are only suggestions. Let your ideas go from here. Keep in mind, though, that if you are to find any real advantage in trading it is not going to be in keeping your tax position identical to what it would be if you were dealing merely in cash.

It is up to you to develop ideas which will work for you, in your situation. It is further necessary to carry out those ideas in a consistent course of action. Learn to be both the fox for cunning and the lion for strength, as Machiavelli advised in his *Prince*. Remember too Thomas Fuller's maxim: *"Boldness in business is the first, second, and third thing."*

Tick off These Important Accounting Points

- To obtain the best accounting advice, select a CPA who understands trading because he is a trader himself.
- Expert opinions vary tremendously as to the accountability of barter transactions for tax purposes—from its being a legal and moral duty to report all trades as if they were cash, to "report nothing!"
- An IRS bulletin to CPAs says "a dollar in trade must be treated no different than if it were cash."
- However, there is no reference to trade-club currencies findable either in IRS informational documents or in the privately issued federal tax guides.
- Certain kinds of trades are taxable but others are nontaxable,

according to the IRS. Regular inventory items are taxable when bartered; non-inventory items, traded like for like, are not.

- One CPA, when asked about how to report trade-club credits, said they're to be handled as if they were promissory notes of no established fair market value. As such, they do not represent income on either the accrual or cash basis until spent.
- Trade credits computerized can be made untraceable by simply erasing stored memories; and at least one major trade club routinely dumps its transaction data when it becomes a year old.
- What's the safest course to follow in accounting for your trade deals? Do exactly as the IRS says is safest; but it is also the dullest and least profitable way to go.
- Alternative suggestion: brainstorm your specific situation after researching relevant data and conferring with your CPA and lawyer. You can no doubt find another course of action which will shelter at least a portion of your barter activity.

Debt is the slavery of the free.—Publilius Syrus

CHAPTER 5

Barter Plus Cash, the Happy Combination

YOU DON'T HAVE TO BE AN EXPERT in order to determine where you stand right now as a trader. You have been bartering all your life, using your personality, your services, your money, and your things as trade goods.

There was a study done once in the psychological field which showed that, among patients released from mental institutions, those with the heaviest case-history files were most likely to be readmitted to the institution.

Some "normal" folks reflect the same findings in their behavior, as measured by various statistical-minded organizations.

Drivers with the thickest files of traffic violations, or accidents, are most likely to have additional ones. Insurance companies know this, and rate drivers accordingly—or refuse their business in severely risky cases.

Citizens with the most negative information in their files at credit-reporting agencies find it difficult or impossible to obtain new credit.

Lenders, insurance carriers, psychologists—even you and I—

know that the best indicator of *future* performance by a person is his performance in *times past.*

The track record we have for handling cash is a pretty good index of how we are likely to handle it in times to come. In turn, the way we view cash, and how we use it to our advantage or disadvantage, is a prime clue to how alert we are as traders. After all, we exchange our goods or services for as much cash as we can. The amount we get in return for what we give is one measure of our skill at interpersonal exchange.

How we control our outflow of cash when we trade for things or services we desire is another measure of our trading ability.

Four Levels of Ability to Use Cash: Where Do You Fit In?

Constant Borrower. Perpetually runs at the limit of bank-card credit or other charge accounts; pays interest on money owed at high rates; frequently borrows on long-term basis to pay current or recurring expenses. Seldom has any cash savings. Converts assets to cash at discounted rates.

Charge-Account Happy. Seldom thinks twice about charging anything needed or desired. Buys routinely at standard retail prices. Does not defer purchases to take advantage of sales or seasonal discounts. Pays bills promptly but seldom has much cash left over for investment. Credit generally used instead of cash; has both bank cards and a dozen other charge cards.

Cash Customer. Has a few of the standard charge cards but seeks ways to get a discount by using cash instead. Asks for discount when paying cash at places he could charge things. Obtains cash discount for buying in quantity. Buys at sales as a matter of policy. Seeks ways to put ready cash to work earning income. A regular saver.

Sharp Buyer. Purchases most large items at or near wholesale. Has established discount sources for most commodities needed for everyday living, including food and clothing. Maintains a reserve stock of almost everything, including cash. Alert for ways to make cash or other resources pay off at rates far better than savings accounts. Credit is triple-A but almost never needs to use it.

If you should happen not to like the spot on this rating scale that describes your use of cash, why not change how you operate? It can be done. Unlike the leopard, human beings *can* remove the spotty portions of their personalities. (Utilize the information in Appendix 3.)

Cash and Trade Goods: They're Both Just Commodities

Your performance in handling cash reflects your general approach to life as a whole. If you find yourself perpetually running into debt, you will notice that along with it your life as a whole is stressful and your personal reserves are at low ebb. Making profitable exchanges at any level of living—business or personal—is difficult or impossible. If you are able to buy sharply, though, that requires you to be put together in good running shape beforehand. You cannot act like a tiger in transactions if you feel like a mouse.

Since money is used so widely in our lives, we tend to think of it as a mysterious thing in itself. Yet it is not. It is no different from other commodities in its tradeability. The daily international money markets, with fluctuating values for the various national currencies, show that it is essentially just another commodity—like hog bellies or soybeans or March eggs.

In the general run of affairs, it is money's *convertibility* which makes it so handy to use. These days, too, money is easy to store.

You can keep a thousand dollars—or a million, for that matter—in a few magnetized traces on a tape or disc.

Money in our modern understanding of it, divorced from precious metals, is unlike other commodities in that it has no usefulness in itself. You can make jewelry or teeth out of gold, for instance. You can eat corn, wear wool, build a house with lumber. Not so money.

Therefore it is well to keep money in good balance in your thinking as a trader. In inflationary times such as those in which we live, money becomes an ever more doubtful commodity to keep on hand. Proof of this may be seen in the rush to buy land as a large-scale investment. On a small scale, just check your neighborhood garage sales. You will find that almost no one will part with *tools*. If some show up, they are the first things sold. Land and the means to work it: unconsciously our better traders are already pointing the way for us to go, in quite consciously seeking their own advantage during times of increasing instability.

Because of its present instability, pay particular attention to how you use money in your trading. When you sell, stay alert to money's diminishing value because of inflation. Enter into long-term contracts (and that may mean only weeks or months) with an eye to adjustments in prices over that period. Don't let yourself get caught selling at fixed rates that become more ridiculously low as the days go by.

When you buy, train yourself to get the most out of your cash. Shop the marketplace for any commodity you need. Learn the facts about the differential in prices, from place to place and time to time. Make it your policy to buy at those places and times where you get the utmost for your cash outlay.

Here's a homely example.

I live in an area rich in forest products. Western Washington exports timber and lumber and related by-products to the world. Because of its availability, wood is used as a supplementary (or even primary) heating fuel by many residents of the area, especially in rural or small-town locations.

I read the classified ads. During the winter months, when heat is imperative, wood has recently sold for $50 to $55 a cord, delivered. You can buy it for $5 or so less if you haul it. If you want it stacked you pay an extra $5 or so.

These prices are for unseasoned wood. Seasoned wood is virtually unobtainable during the winter months.

Spring and summer prices are a lot less: $35 to $40 a cord, sometimes stacked as part of the deal. By the next winter, such wood is seasoned and burns with much more heat than when green.

So you'd say that the smart buyer lays in his five or six cords of wood during the warm season, at reduced rates, and is sitting pretty when the arctic blasts begin to blow.

Well, maybe.

It is possible to do better than that. There is a local company that manufactures telephone poles. These are specially selected treetrunks, peeled, smoothed and otherwise trued up. They are finished to certain diameters and lengths.

However, nature grows the trees any lengths it pleases, so the men trim off a foot or two from this pole, three or four from that one, in order to standardize them to match their orders.

The pole company workyard is littered with these remnant pieces on days when the men have been cutting the poles to length.

Bill King and his wife, Maureen, are traders. They run an answering service (they take calls for me on a trade-out basis) and Bill is also in the insurance business. The Kings explained the pole company's operation to me.

"Call 'em up to find out when they have been cutting," advised Bill. "Then plan to take your pickup over there just at twelve o'clock. That's the lunch hour, and you won't get in the men's way. Go prowling around the yard, looking on the ground for cut-off pieces. Toss 'em in your pickup. On the way out, stop at the office and pay five dollars for your pickup load.

"When you get 'em home, get out your chain saw and cut the ones that are too long down to stovewood length. Stack your wood up and it'll be seasoned by the time you need it. Run over there every few weeks during the summer and you'll be all set to heat your house in the winter."

A pickup truck, half-ton size, can haul just about half a cord of unseasoned wood at a trip. Multiply it out, and you find that a handy trader could by this means tuck away his year's heating wood at $10 a cord. That's quite a reduction off the rates previously discussed, and no doubt well worth the extra effort required for someone with a pickup truck and a chain saw. (Of course in communities such as this, every householder is a trader to some degree, and most homes have a half-ton or mini pickup parked outside as a matter of trading necessity.)

You are beginning to understand the price differential of the marketplace, I hope. However, there is more.

A homeowner in these parts can also get a permit (free) which entitles him to cut up to six cords of wood for his own use out of designated portions of government forest land.

So if you want to throw in a little additional work, you can get all the wood you'll need for winter heating at no cost except your time and effort.

That's getting right down to the sharp edge of economics. Still, it is possible to go a step farther with this.

John Casey is a lawyer of my acquaintance, a trader in general and a trade-club member in particular. John loves the rural life, and has his house plumped down in the middle of substantial acreage not far from town. This includes a woodlot.

"I sell my services, cash or trade, at fifty dollars an hour," John told me. "That gives me pretty good leverage in trading for other services. So I hire most of the work around my place done, using artisans and handymen from my trade club as much as I can. I get all my winter heating wood cut using trade credits, paying top rate of about seven dollars in credits per hour. So I get the whole heating problem taken care of for a couple of hours of my time and a little trading savvy." That leaves John with his cash intact to spend on other things, or to invest. Not a bad deal.

Even if he were not the owner of a piece of wooded land, John could still hire someone else to cut on his (John's) permit off the government forest land. Nor would he pay 79¢ a bundle for kindling.[1]

So keep shopping yourself for better deals in the marketplace, using your trading skills to maximize what you obtain for either trade credits, commodities, services or cash. It will reward you richly to do so. You don't need to live in a rural community, nor in a forested area, to benefit from the uneven balance of the marketplace. Wherever you live there are equivalent opportunities, although some communities provide more of certain kinds of opportunities than others. It depends far more on *who and what you are* than it does on *where you are*.

How a Little Cash Can Produce Big Trading Profits

Our next chapter will give many more examples, but let me tell you how Larry and Jill Erwin operate.

Larry is a scenic painter, and makes his own frames. Jill sells jewelry. (She doesn't make it, but buys through wholesale chan-

[1] Further investigation reveals that a person in this community can get all the kindling wood he wants delivered free. All he needs to do is call one of the shake mills in the area, who will bring him a gigantic truckload of odd-size waste pieces of cedar shakes and dump it in his yard. At the same time, the supermarkets sell little bundles of kindling (weighing at most a couple of pounds) for 79¢ in the winter, 49¢ in the summer. That's the price differential of the marketplace illustrated in fluorescent paint.

nels and selects attractive merchandise with the usual long markup potential.)

Larry's only cost is in his materials and time. He is willing to trade his framed subjects for straight barter, with no cash required. Since he's a recognized artist with a following, he can demand his full retail prices when he trades—several hundred dollars a picture. Jill, with a larger cash outlay for her jewelry items, is in a different position. When she trades she asks 50 percent in cash when trading within a trade club for trade credits which, as we have already seen, are discounted to begin with.

Both Larry and Jill sell most of their products for straight cash, but when they trade they also do very well. Minor cash makes Larry's products easy to trade. More cash leaves Jill's items tradeable, but returns her investment in cash. That's the best of both worlds.

Red Lights Flash When the Other Trader Asks for Cash, Too

It's usually advantageous for you if you can *get* cash as well as trade goods or services when you let your merchandise or skills go.

Beware, though, when the other trader starts asking for cash in return. Inspect his merchandise very carefully to make sure that you couldn't duplicate it using cash alone, for no more than the money he wants not including your trade goods.

It depends upon how sharp you are, how much effort and time you are willing to spend finding other sources, how much you want the article in question, and how much total expenditure you're contemplating, whether you will decide to give up cash as well as trade goods when the other party asks for it.

Keep in mind the facts of the marketplace—the cash marketplace—when you are negotiating barter deals. If it becomes important enough, because of the size of the transaction, shop to see what you can do for cash only. You may want only one item, and a single unit of that. It may not pay to go any further than the trader who has it and wants a little cash too. You may need more items, or a quantity of one item. Then you can be pretty sure that it will pay you to shop for an all-cash deal.

In case you've never given much thought to it, there's an eye-opening education awaiting you when you start investigating sources of items you want to buy for less cash.

There's a continuum of pricing. It runs from Suggested Retail (or even more) at one end, to Distress Merchandise at the other. At the low end you can plan on buying for immediate cash at about ten cents of the going retail dollar. That's when you buy directly from the owner who desperately needs money, can't hold on to his property, or wants out for other reasons.

Next to that is the specialist in closeout merchandise. You may have to haggle with him, but if you know his buying price you can generally offer him a fair profit and still do well yourself. (Remember, he *buys* at about ten cents on the dollar, so doubling his money is a fair markup.)

Then there's the manufacturer's closeout price, which may be at about the specialist's price for general merchandise. Next to this is the manufacturer's price to his largest distributors (well below wholesale). Still higher are manufacturer's prices to less-favored distributors, followed in turn by wholesale prices. Next come wholesale-plus-percent discounters, followed by the several levels of regular retail discounters. At the top are standard retailers and their so-called standard prices, with the higher-priced specialty stores and boutiques selling at a premium on that.

There's the situation.

It all depends on you and your skill in ferreting out real buys for cash when that is important to you. You may be able to obtain the same (or at least equivalent) merchandise for a fraction of what you might have expected to pay—if you seek it out and bargain for your price and terms.

Knowing all this, walk around a deal a few times before saying yes when the other trader wants cash plus merchandise. If you give it to him what you're doing is paying him in cash for what the thing cost him, with all the rest of the trade thrown in as "boot." It may save you trouble to do it. It may be a good deal. But it may not be, so be wary.

Be Fair to Others but Don't Be a Victim

It takes a good bit of time and trouble, usually, to work out a really low-priced deal. Much of the time it may not be worth it to do so. Your specific situation will determine how much time for or interest in bargain hunting you have.

However much of it you do, let me say a word in caution. Don't push a good thing too far. Don't always seek the last penny's advantage. It pays to be fair—both for your sake and that of the other party in the trade, and for the benefit of the trading community in general.

While you may be on a perpetual lookout for people who don't want what they have, or can't afford to keep it, or who have outworn or outgrown it, because these are fertile prospects for lucrative trading, most of your transactions will be on a more one-for-one basis.

Having gone to the trouble of finding a trader you can deal with, it pays you to let him have a profit too . . . if you intend to do business with him regularly. And you will want to establish regular trading relationships, because it's a drag trying to find someone who has what you want when you really need it. It's much easier if you have such a source already, nourished by profit-making barter deals with you in times past. So be fair with your regular trading buddies. Make them your friends.

You also owe it to yourself, to other traders, and to the trading field in general, not to let yourself be ripped off by sharpsters.

No matter whether the amount is large or small, make sure that you are being treated fairly in each transaction. If you let yourself be had, it may set a pattern for what you expect trading to be like. Thereafter each transaction may just seem to work out so you get the short end of the trade. Over time you may become disgruntled and irked at the very idea of barter or working out a deal with someone who is also a trader.

Or your one first big loss at trading may set you so much against the whole idea that you never again will get into negotiations with anyone.

In either instance, you become a permanently impaired transactor of trade exchanges; you express your negativities to others; gradually you spoil trading all about you.

You thereby shut down opportunities for yourself and others. (I mentioned some members in trade clubs who spread their gloom throughout the whole interchange network. Save yourself from becoming one of them!)

You'll never become suspicious and sour in that fashion if you keep your eyes open and do not permit yourself to be cheated.

That performs another useful function, too, of benefit to all the traders around you. By refusing to be taken in by sharpies, you make it harder for them to make their tactics work. It discourages them. You do not reinforce their larcenous ideas by letting them succeed.

It boils down to this: You count. Your actions are important. The bigger and better you become as a trader, the more influence you have. Live fairly yourself and see to it that others do likewise.

Take Another Look at These Cash/Barter Ideas

- How we handle our cash is a good estimate of our ability as traders.

- Check *your* category: ( ) I am at the limit of my charge accounts, need to borrow; ( ) I use my charge accounts freely for standard-priced goods; ( ) I prefer to use cash and ask for discounts; ( ) I buy major items at wholesale, have low-cost sources for other items. (If you don't like your rating spot as a cash-user, change by using the information in Appendix 3.)
- Money is like other commodities in that its price rises and falls.
- Money is unlike other commodities since you can't eat it or wear it or use it for anything else.
- Get the most out of your money by shopping carefully.
- Learn the facts about the price differential: costs in the marketplace vary from place to place and time to time for identical goods or services.
- No matter where you live, exceptional bargains are available if you look for them.
- Though every community is different in its special kinds of opportunities, *who and what you are* is more important than *where you are.*
- It's more profitable for you if you can get both cash and commodities or services when you barter.
- Therefore a red light should pop on when the *other* trader asks for cash as well as trade goods.
- There's a continuum of pricing on equivalent items, which runs from a high of Suggested Retail or higher, down to Distress Merchandise that sells at about 10 percent of normal retail.
- When you find a trader you can exchange with, let him profit too so that you can trade with him again.
- Don't rip off other traders; don't let them rip you off: thus you keep the barter business a pleasant one for everyone.

There are few ways in which a man can be more in-
nocently employed than in getting money.
—Samuel Johnson

CHAPTER 6

Cashing Out on Your Own
Barter Deals

YOU HAVE ALREADY COME TO LOOK UPON MONEY—cash—as
just one more commodity. At least I hope you have, for when you
begin to learn how to turn trade goods into cash you need to look
on money that way. It is not something different in *kind* from
other items of trade. Money is simply different *in detail.*

"Think of us as your money store," runs the happy slogan of
one banking chain seeking borrowers. That tells much of the
story.

Money can be bought. Every time you perform a service for it,
or trade merchandise for it, you *buy* the money with what you
give up.

Money can be rented. When you take out a loan from a bank
or other lender, you are renting the use of the money. Something
like a drive-it-yourself automobile you borrow from a rent-a-car
operator, you use the money for an agreed-to time. Then you return it. And you pay for your use of the commodity.

Money is convenient. Therein lies its greatest temptation to
misuse. Yet there also is the clue to developing your success in
barter.

If you learn to use money as a special kind of commodity, and at the same time shape up your other trading skills, you can find ways to convert a little money into much trade goods—and much trade goods back into a lot more money than you began with.

It requires skill to seek out and set up transactions that will pay off in cash. This you develop by practice. It takes patience not to cash out at the first opportunity, and realize a loss or little profit. Patience comes as you mellow into a philosophical trader who can take the good and the bad of the world in stride and await just *the* right time.

More than this, cashing out on your trades successfully means being willing to make concessions in ultimate value in exchange for the convenience and general utility of cash. Here's a general rule:

Cash to Barter—Demand More
Barter to Cash—Take Less

Don't take the rule so much to heart that you *insist* on it, even if the other fellow doesn't know about it. But keep it in mind.

This is merely an extension of the general principle at work in all aspects of trade and commerce, that certain commodities are more desired than others by most people. From that stems their reluctance to give them up unless for an obviously equivalent value. And related to this rule, when the transaction is looked at from the other side, of their willingness to give more in order to obtain the preferred item.

The general rule just cited applies with greatest aptness when you are dealing in commodities of accepted value in money.

As an example, take automobiles. Cars selling at list prices of several thousands of dollars apiece are costly to keep on the dealer's lot. He pays rent on the money tied up in his inventory;

the longer he keeps a given auto, the more it costs him. And these costs come out of his profit margin on the car.

All these factors are weighing the scales in favor of someone— you, perhaps—who comes with a desire for a specific car on the dealer's floor and ready cash.

The dealer frequently will take less in total dollars—or give more in accessories—if he needs the money.

Quite the opposite is true, of course, when there are occasional shortages of cars (or any other commodity). The seller then can demand more money for the car, and get it. But that is because the scales have shifted; the balance is now on the dealer's side. The car becomes more valuable than the cash.

Most of the time, in our society, there is an ample supply of most commodities. Hence the general application of our rule. But be alert for the exceptions—shift to commodities rather than cash whenever it seems feasible to do so.

Here's a funny incident that illustrates perfectly the principle of converting a little cash into a lot of barter—and back into a lot of cash.

The 50¢ Used Book That Sold for $170 Trade and $84 Cash

Carl and Harriet are a congenial middle-aged couple who enjoy life and its creative aspects. Harriet paints; Carl is good with tools. Both have a knack for trading. Harriet is a great bargain-finder. Carl is excellent at getting the ultimate value from them.

One day Harriet came home from shopping and dropped a surprise gift in Carl's lap.

"I picked it up at a garage sale, hon," she told him. "The man had a lot of stuff that had been rained on, but I spent 50¢ on this book for you even if the pages are wet and sort of warped from the rain."

"This," as Carl told me the story later, was a paper-covered book of lithographed reproductions of bawdy 18th-century English prints. The quality of the reproductions was poor, but the racy humor of the originals made up for that. All in all, there were 67 prints in the book, Carl said. Thirteen were monotones in black and greys. The remaining 54 were in color.

"After our first laugh together, Harriet and I put our heads to work on how to convert our little book into a modest profit," Carl told me. And here, in brief, is what they did.

The first creative act was to see the book in terms of its appeal not just to one buyer, but to many. So they pulled the damp volume apart and turned it into individual prints.

Harriet improved the quality of these tremendously by taking an iron to them, steaming them a bit here and there and generally getting them flattened out.

Then Carl took over. He invested another $14 and change in mat board for mounting the prints. He chose colors harmonious with the main color themes of the pictures. He had them cut to a convenient size by the art-supply dealer he bought them from.

One weekend he spent a couple of hours trimming the prints evenly and cementing them to the boards. Finally he cut up a corrugated carton into an appropriate shape for a little storage bin, which he covered outside with walnut-grain Contac paper.

Then he took his little self-display merchandiser kit to the next trade fair held by one of his trade clubs.

"I made two mistakes in my estimate of what would happen," Carl related ruefully. "I priced the matted-up prints in trade units at the equivalent of $15 each. That was way too high. And I overestimated the interest the traders at the fair would have in that kind of material."

For whatever reason, that day Carl sold only one picture.

But he learned his lesson, cut the price, and went to another trade bazaar catering to a younger and more with-it crowd.

"I sold 'em as singles, I priced 'em in pairs, and wound up the day with only 23 left. All told, I came out with $170 in trade units."

That wasn't too bad, considering that this was merely a side issue. Carl and Harriet were really concentrating on moving her paintings. They realized many hundreds of trade dollars for their efforts with them.

But Carl wasn't satisfied. He still had 23 prints in his little display case, and wanted to cash out on his investment.

This he did shortly afterward.

He related how Harriet, in her careful daily scrutiny of the newspaper, one day shortly after the second trade fair clipped two ads and put them on the arm of his chair. Both were for the same auction company.

A small ad said "Antiques, Bric-a-Brac Wanted for Auction." It gave a location and date. The large ad, for the same time and place, was the announcement of an auction of valuable oriental rugs.

"Apparently they wanted the smaller stuff as a crowd-builder for the carpets," Carl said. "Anyway, we took in a few other things we had *and* the 23 remaining pictures."

Every one of the erotic prints sold, though some of their other items did not. Net after commission to the auction house: $84.00 to Carl and Harriet.

Now that's no tremendous deal—the amounts are quite small. But the *method* involved is very important to learn for successful cash-out in trading.

The elements are:

- Be alert for bargains, even if somewhat distressed in quality. (It's amazing what a little refurbishing can do.)
- Let your creative juices flow. Plan how to get the maximum possible (cash or trade) out of what you have obtained inexpensively.

- Ask yourself, Who would be able to use this? In what form, place, manner should I offer it?
- What would it bring just as it is, under the right conditions?
- What can I do to increase its apparent value and saleability? (That means by cleaning, mounting, wrapping, painting, and the like.)
- Having decided what to do, then go ahead with your plan. If it seems worthwhile, invest a reasonable amount of time and money (or trade services or products) to bring it to a successful conclusion.

That brings up a salient point in learning to trade:

Creativity Pays Off in Turning Barter into Cash

This is not some wise saying, such as "Honesty is the best policy" or "All work and no play makes jack." It is really the key to making *any* trade deal successful. Or any cash deal, for that matter.

And creativity can be learned.

Keep looking at your stock in trade, or some service you can render, in terms of the points mentioned a few lines earlier.

Train yourself in the habit of seeing the ultimate *use* of what you have rather than merely what it is at the moment.

The man with a damp book who sold it for 50¢ to Harriet saw it merely as a damp book that might have cost him $10 in the first place. He was happy to cash out in terms of his creativity. (Better 50¢ in hand than a mouldy book in the trash can!)

But Harriet and Carl could see more in the book than that. And they proceeded to extract both trade credits and cash out of it in terms of their vision.

Trading enhances this kind of creativity. Here are more instances, each the actual experience of a skilled barterer well known to me. Each case is authentic.

The Bartered Roll of Paper that Turned
into 10,000 Sketch Pads

Jack Hensley sells materials to stores who specialize in graphic arts materials. He also sells to businesses who use such items, and to schools and other institutions.

He is also a canny trader.

Over coffee one day he told me a story that reflects his ability—especially his creativity.

In looking for other things one day in the corner of a paper junkyard he came across a roll (such as webfed offset presses use) of white paper. Casually working his way around to the subject with the yard owner, he finally wound up trading some vacation scrip for the roll. Before leaving, Jack tore off a length of stock from the roll and later that day put it into the hands of an artist friend of his.

"Tell me what this paper is good for in the graphic arts field," Jack requested. "I've got to have that roll of paper picked up within a day or two, and I need to know what I'm going to do with it."

The artist spent a little while working on the sample with pencils, pens, felt brushes, pastels, water colors and perhaps even acrylics. His report was succinct. "Jack, that stuff is almost as porous as blotting paper. The only thing it's good for is the roughest kind of sketching."

Jack thanked him, and none dismayed had the several-hundred-pound roll trucked over to a converter nearby and had it slitted into sheets. Then it was made up into pads with a colored sheet as a cover and a chipboard back.

Jack took samples of these 1417 pads around on his calls to his customers. He had the pads priced somewhat under other sketch pads (he could afford to!) and within a week he'd sold the entire batch.

Jack didn't tell me the value of the scrip he'd traded for the roll of paper, but I'd guess it might have been worth $150 or so if you'd put a cash price on it.

Nor did he tell me exactly what he sold the pads for, nor exactly how many there were. But he did say, when I asked about the quantity of finished pads he got out of the roll, "Gosh, I forget—but it must have been ten thousand or so."

I still have my tongue in cheek about *ten thousand* pads. But it could easily have been two or three thousand.

I'd guess they'd retail at about $2.00 each, which meant $1.20 or so in cash each for Jack. Total sale: Somewhere between $2,400 and $3,600.

Not bad for the very simple creative act of visualizing the big junked roll of paper converted into something saleable. And carrying through with the other steps necessary.

And banking the sizeable cash-out from what began as barter.

The Bartered Lot with the Gaping Hole and the Buyer Who Asked for More

People who are active traders in real estate often exchange lots and acreage they never see. Such properties form a currency of a sort, and pass from trader to trader at whatever the current deal will bear in terms of dollar valuation.

But every once in awhile the buyer of a piece of this kind of property gets curious. He wants to go see just what he bought.

Tom is a very well known, highly successful trader.

On his way back from a trip to Texas he stopped to look at some acreage he'd recently acquired through trading.

He drove out to the place and, much to his consternation, found that it neatly surrounded a tremendous hole in the ground. You couldn't build on the land. You couldn't run cattle on it. Worthless.

Except that Tom began ruminating on the hole. Instead of

wasting his time angrily recriminating the person who'd traded the land to him, he put his creativity to work.

When he told me the story, he was laughing about it.

"I began to ask myself, 'Who needs a hole?' and pretty soon I realized that a *trash service* needs someplace to dump its loads of waste material. So I hunted up a trash-service operator and sold him my hole."

Tom and I were both laughing at the ridiculous story.

"The deal went through, everybody was happy, and I forgot about it. But then, a couple of years later, I got a call from the man who'd bought it for a dump site. He wanted to buy another one just like it!"

We don't need to inquire as to how much profit Tom converted his property into. I'm sure he did well in that regard—he usually does.

The remarkable thing about this incident is the quick recovery, turning sure disaster into a positive value, characteristic of a creative trader.

How Bill Allen Turns $1,000 Cash into $10,000

Bill Allen is a big, friendly, direct-talking man whose special area of operation is buying entire drugstores that are moving or going out of business, then selling the stock at a profit . . . a *handsome* profit.

The $1,000 and $10,000 figures are mine, not Bill's. But they reflect the *proportion* of cost to selling price quite accurately. Bill is far too experienced a trader to pay more than 10¢ on the dollar for distress merchandise.

Then the fun begins.

Bill reopens the same drugstore, if it is available to him, and runs a close-out sale at 50 per cent off. For cash.

He utilizes circulars and the community shopping newspaper

for advertising. Within a couple of weeks he has made a bundle.

Then frequently he will open the store once more for a one-day extravaganza for members of one of the trading clubs he belongs to.

This time, for trade credits, he sells everything at full list price. He makes another bundle in trade chits. (And he knows how to spend them effectively too.)

Finally he takes the remaining merchandise, combines it with other stock, and sells it through a half-price close-out store he rents specifically for that purpose in a low-rent location off a main avenue.

He hires inexpensive help to operate the store, and gradually sells off (or trades for other needed items) the remaining merchandise.

Bill and his wife live very well. They have a second home at the shore. They travel. (The last time they were in England they toured much of the country on credits arranged with an English barter organization.)

And all this happens because Bill can see a creative solution to someone's else need to close up or move a business.

You may be able to do something similar in a line you are well acquainted with.

Now Let's Go over the Trade-to-Cash Techniques Again

- Money is a commodity, like anything else. You can rent it, you can buy it.
- Money is also convenient. That makes it easy to misuse.
- Be willing to make concessions in cashing-out on barter deals—take less than face value of your merchandise if necessary. (But don't *plan* it that way!)
- Get into the habit of looking at your trade-into-cash situation

creatively. Learn to spot bargains. Ask yourself who would be able to use the item in question as it is, or as you can modify or improve it. What price would it bring?

- When you decide to work your plan, then carry it out.
- The same principles apply whether you're dealing with paper, real estate, merchandise or anything else.

What we have to learn to do, we learn by doing.
—Aristotle

CHAPTER 7

The How-To of Heads-Up Barter
Made Easy

FRED DEAN IS THE THIRD GENERATION to operate Dean's Drug Store in Tacoma, and a highly successful trader for cash as well as kind.

"My grandfather started this business in 1921," Fred told me, "and in those days the whole business community was concentrated in a few square blocks of the downtown section.

"All the merchants and professional people knew each other, they ate lunch at the same places, worked for the same civic improvements, traded with each other as a matter of friendship and convenience.

"Every month they'd get together and settle up who owed what to balance accounts. Nobody had very much money, but everyone lived well because they'd trade for what they wanted.

"For instance, my other grandfather was a doctor, and in those days doctors, like all other professional men, had to take produce in order to get paid. He took in enough lumber to build two houses.

"But times have changed. There's more money around now, for one thing, and people have become used to paying with money for things they used to have to trade for.

"Then too, business has spread out to the malls and the suburban shopping areas, so that the merchants and professional people have lost that personal contact they used to have. There isn't the easy opportunity to trade that there used to be.

"Yet the person in business who wants to get ahead just about has to trade in order to get the most out of his money. That means going after the trading opportunities that once were a matter of daily routine."

A trade club, says Dean, is one good way of facilitating contacts with other traders. So is getting to know your customers as people, when they come to do business with you for cash. That can often lead to a big trading opportunity, far beyond the small purchase they stopped in for. And another good method of pursuing trading opportunities is by telephone, following up chance leads, prospecting, or asking friends (or even strangers) if they're open to trade for what you want.

I'd guess Fred Dean is a pretty good trader. He has a prosperous business. He is in the midst of putting $40,000 worth of remodeling work into a mansion that came to him by inheritance—almost all of the materials and labor through trading. Fred Dean's trading advice is based upon personal experience, and agrees in every particular with the barter philosophy I have heard from dozens of other traders.

You'll be able to detect echoes of Fred's story throughout the next several chapters, for his experiences are similar to those of other business owners and professionals everywhere. Their problems are similar; the solutions, too, are similar.

One to One, the O-o-o-nly Way to Trade

Ultimately, even when you use cash or trade credits, barter exchanges come down to one person working out a deal with another. Even if in today's gone-mad society most purchases are not this way, still it remains the better method to get to know the person you are trading with as a human being.

If you reflect on it for yourself, you'll see reasons why this is so. To get you started, I'll spell out a few of them:

- When you get to know the other party personally in trading, the likelihood diminishes that he will cheat you in any way. He stands in the transaction right with his merchandise.
- Knowing the other party makes it possible to enlarge the scope of your trading—to include other items, or to make it a continuing process every month or every season. That saves you time in setting up other trading relationships.
- Having the other trader get to know you as a willing and honest barter partner will likewise open the door for him to offer wider opportunities to you. These may be his own requirements, or may be the needs of his friends who in turn want to trade their goods or services for what you have to offer.

This can be summarized by saying:

Make It Easy—Trade Where You're Known

Fred Dean's description of trading in the business community of two or three generations ago illustrates the first principle of barter. Trade where you are already known, where your merchandise or services are established in quality, and where you have earned a reputation for fair dealing and honest value.

Trading of this kind can begin as small as you wish, no matter where you are. Youngsters trade picture cards, marbles and comic books—not with strangers, but with the kids next door or across the street.

Housewives exchange babysitting with each other, or swap a batch of cookies for dressmaking help, or simply trade recipes and gossip.

People in business routinely do this if they are long established in their communities, but not so much on goods and services as on help with outside projects. Yet making trades of ordinary items on a daily or weekly basis builds business and reputations faster than the concentration on mere dollar transactions can do. Such cash deals today are faceless, for the most part. Checks pass each other in the mail. Voices on the telephone have no human features attached to them. Computers chatter away in their electronic nonsense patter and millions of value units shift from one account to another—at the expense of human contacts.

Trading builds a sense of shared realities, accents the human qualities of exchange and the goods or services involved. Even if you trade with others remote in distance, your sense of friendly interest, each for the other, grows. In the same city, or same building complex, trading makes friends even more easily. That's where to begin.

Trading with neighbors is so natural it takes no skill.

A few years ago I had an office in a large office building. I frequently needed small quick-print jobs run off, and worked out a trade arrangement with Izzy Bick, who had the suite next to mine, to run my stuff off on his little office offset machine. In exchange I supplied him with help in his promotion and other writing.

There was a school on the next floor, selling courses across the country by mail. I offered help with some of their writing needs and in exchange obtained extensive help with information about schools, for some other things I was writing at the time.

I traded a couple of pictures with the ticket agency down the hall, which in turn supplied me with a desk it no longer needed but was essential for one of my rooms.

Some shelving came my way from a travel agency on an upper

floor, for which I prepared copy for a piece of promotion literature they needed, and we were both happy.

These little trades from my own experience are nothing great; they are everyday occurrences if you are open to them and merely look about you wherever you happen to be located.

They have three great advantages: they get you what you want; they build friendly relationships with neighbors; and they save you cash.

Make it a practice, when you need something, to think first in terms of how you can get it *without cash*. That will lead you directly to our next step in heads-up trading:

Shape Your Offer, Refine It—and Offer!

The trader who creates the offer is in a position similar to that of the person who writes the contract—he sets it up to suit himself, including his estimate of what it will take for the other party to respond with a yes.

You don't necessarily have to go out seeking trades; you can wait for them to come to you. (If you have a reputation as a barterer, and your services or goods are in demand, other traders will seek you out. That's the case with people such as Jim Yeats, the jeweler I mentioned in Chapter 2.)

Nonetheless, if you are just starting out as a trader, you will be well rewarded to seek out others with whom to trade. Your wait for them to come to you might be a long one otherwise.

The six steps in formulating an offer to trade run like this:

1. You have a service to render, or merchandise to exchange, with a value in the general marketplace which you can establish.
2. You have a desire for another piece of goods, or kind of service, of roughly equivalent value.

3. You search your mind, assisted by the phone book or even inquiries in the business world, for someone who regularly does that kind of work or sells that sort of item.
4. You mentally weigh all the factors, then you go to see the person you have chosen to suggest a trade to.
5. You add a little plus-value in your offer—"boot"—to make the deal more acceptable to the other party. (*Enticement* might be the better word, as it frequently turns out.)[1]
6. Then you simply state what you have, and that you wish to exchange it for the thing the other person has and which you name.

The boot often takes the form of just words. Here are a few examples. Note how they tend to clinch the deal, yet cost nothing.

Bill Allen, mentioned in the previous chapter, used this technique with the artist who put together the paste-ups of ads for him: The artist was giving him dubious looks about doing the job, which Bill wanted right away . . . so Bill said, "Look, it can be *rough*." The artist took this to mean that he could bang it out with less time than usual, hence with greater profit to himself.

Dal Nichols, the restaurateur profiled in Chapter 2, ran into some resistance with the carpet cleaner he wanted to service his establishment: "Your meals are too big, and my wife and I are both on diets." Dal's reply was, "I'll honor the trade-out with your friends or customers; you can take care of your Christmas gifts that way." The deal was accepted.

Ken Peddicord, who with his wife Jeannette runs a business-machine repair and sales business in Bellevue, near Seattle, uses this same tactic. "Buy the copier, and I'll throw in this paper," he said to a potential purchaser of a used Thermofax machine. (Of course Ken had taken in the paper along with the copier, so the boot amounted to words.)

[1] Some traders also use the word "vigorish," which means something more than a tip but less than a bribe.

If Ken had said, "Take the machine and I'll give you six months' free service on it," that would have been true boot . . . if there had been any reason to actually make a service call on the equipment.

And it is boot if the camera enthusiast offers to trade the camera, then as a clincher throws in the camera case (or the light meter, or filters, etc.).

Formulate what you're willing to give; settle on what you want in exchange; then make your offer.

Experienced traders like to go in person to make their trade negotiations. Reason? It is harder for the other person to say no to a live body physically present than it is to reject a proposal made by the relatively remote phone instrument.

Be willing to go yourself, as necessary, to work out your deals.

The Peddicords are fine examples of the experienced trader at work. With their kind permission, I'll relate some of their activities here.

Both Ken and Jeannette are skilled technicians, and spend many of their working hours in the field.

"We're always prospecting," says Ken. "When we finish a repair job or service call, we stop in at the places nearby to find out if they need our services for cash. That pays our bread and butter."

"We're also active members of a trade club," adds Jeannette. "Their business—from other members—is good because it's plus business we wouldn't otherwise get. It also leads to referrals outside the trade club, which means added cash volume."

Ken points out the value of trade-ins. "It adds equipment to our inventory which we acquire without having to lay out cash." He did not mention it, but such deals probably mean a double profit-margin, too: one on the servicing and repairing of the traded-in machine, the other the normal profit any retailer would expect on merchandise sold.

"We sometimes repair equipment and take another machine as

payment," comments Ken. "Last fall we had a customer who wasn't sure whether it was worthwhile to have us rework a pair of old typewriters. So we traded our repair service on one machine, taking the other one as our payment.

"Another one of our customers is an artist whose son was going away to college and needed a typewriter. But she was strapped for cash to buy him one. We traded her the rebuilt machine we had previously taken in for three of her paintings. Then we used the paintings as major gifts on our Christmas list."

"Another customer runs a department store," relates Jeannette. "He wanted a big new Rolodex to keep his master list of customers on. That piece of equipment costs around two hundred and fifty dollars and we didn't have one. But we discovered just the unit we needed in a bunch of stuff being closed out by another business. The Rolodex was unused, but covered with dust. The cards were brand-new and had never been unwrapped. We picked up the thing at no great price, and cleaned it up carefully. Then we traded it to our department store owner for one hundred dollars in merchandise.

"That made us all happy. Our customer received the equivalent of a two hundred and fifty dollar piece of equipment for his wholesale cost of the goods we selected in exchange—probably fifty dollars or sixty dollars. We came out with a long profit too."

Those kinds of trades come about because the parties are known to each other, they make their wants evident, they offer something of substantial value in return, they are flexible as to details, and they are concerned that the other party be satisfied also.

You can go and do likewise. Just package your offer, know what you want, select a likely trading partner from whom you can get it, and make your offer.

If any step in this process stops you or slows you down, look at the underlying causes inside *you* and deal with them as outlined in Appendix 3.

Trading's a Two-Way Street that Has Two Sides

"A good conscience is a continual feast," said Robert Burton in his *Anatomy of Melancholy.*

You will have a good conscience when you treat other people with fairness and integrity. You are entitled to a profit, and a good one; but sell good merchandise and deliver skilled service for it.[2] If you do not, your trading will dwindle. What's more, you will have hurt the name of barter in your community and thus will have injured other traders too.

It may pay you to see trading and barter in their historical perspective. In the late Middle Ages, when Europe was a patchwork of tiny warring states, the principal unifying threads were the common religion—that of the Roman church—and trading.

The Europeans craved the spices, perfumes, and silks of the East. The Eastern peoples admired the furs and artifacts of the Europeans. Across a thousand leagues of sea the sailors of the Hanseatic cities plowed their way in tiny vessels laden with treasure—toward the East with one kind of goods, homeward into the setting sun with another.

The merchants of Venice did likewise, following the course laid down by the Romans, the Greeks and Carthaginians, the Phoenicians, and even the ancients of the golden Minoan age.

[2] As you become more experienced in trading, you will learn the rule of thumb that governs legitimate markups to determine the recovery of cost, necessary overhead expenses, and profits. Very simply, the lower the price and the less frequent the exchange, the higher the markup you must add in order to show any profit at all. On the other side of this, the greater volume you are doing, the less markup you will need for a generous profit and thus the lower the price you will be able to charge. The beginning trader (read beginning business entrepreneur) will usually have a marginally successful operation, with few trades in a given period. He must then, to realize a profit, search out special situations and long-profit-potential goods. As he grows in experience, and his volume of trading expands, he can adjust his merchandise acquisition as well as his profit percentage so that he buys from standard sources at normal prices and uses a trade-average markup to give him an even better total profit.

Across the arid wastes of the Near East, too, the heavily laden camels ("ships of the desert") plodded their waterless way in endless precious caravans of silk, gold, spices, ivory, and jewels.

These traders dared dangers of the deep, the menace of pirates, and the threat of thirst and robbers by land, for one thing; *profits.*

And despite distance and danger, regardless of differences of tongue and culture, they succeeded *because their goods were also profitable to their trading partners* in those faraway lands at earth's end.

So make up your mind that if you wish to be a trader there must be enough profit in the transaction to make it worthwhile *for you.* At the same time, the exchange must be profitable for the other party as well. If not, there will be no trading.

"Cheat me in the price," said Thomas Fuller, "but not in the goods." Make a profit—even a long one—but make sure the other person is well served by the exchange also.

The traffic in goods and services flows both ways in the arteries of commerce; and especially so in head-to-head trading. This avenue to riches has two sides—yours and your trader-partner's.

Take away the potential of profit (by serving up poor services or merchandise) and the flow stops. You are then like the movie set of a busy street after the players have gone; it is a mere facade, without life, unpeopled, and needed by no one.

Four Case Histories of Heads-Up Trades

These personal incidents are brief; they involve a single trade only. They are all trades I was personally involved in.

The ability to write, and to do research, is one of my skills, so that kind of service on my part shows up in each of these trades.

One morning, while I was writing an earlier part of this book, I was interrupted by a telephone call.

"I'm Phil Kratzer, and I specialize in cleaning carpets," said the voice on the other end. "I wonder whether I could trade you carpet and upholstery cleaning for your professional help in putting a circular together so I can advertise my business better."

We got together later that day. Details were discussed. A few days after that my home had beautifully steamed-and-vacuumed carpets and Phil had his circular back from the printer. We were both pleased with the results of our trade, which amounted to perhaps $150 in retail price on either side. So were our wives.

Phil's wife told me a couple of weeks later: "We're getting much better response from the new circular than we did from the old one."

My wife said to me: "It's sure great to be able to walk on the carpet again in my bare feet."

All from a need, a phone call, and the necessary follow-through.

The second trade occurred shortly after we moved to the Pacific Northwest, and the quiet of small-town life, after decades in metropolitan centers.

One day I picked up the first dummy issue of a publication called *Northwest Exchange*, a barter newspaper. Its publication office was not too many miles north of where I was living. So I called the editor and outlined my background as a trader, a writer, and a promotion specialist.

A few days later we met at a convenient halfway point, enjoyed coffee and a long conversation. As a result, Carol Colman, the editor, did a profile on me as a trader for the next issue, and I agreed to write a column each issue in exchange for ad space.

An obviously profitable transaction for each party.

A couple of years ago my wife and I and a friend spent a long weekend at Paramount Lodge, at Big Bear Lake in Southern California. Ed Noonan and I got to discussing his needs for the hotel/cabins property he owned and operated; he told me he wanted to issue his own hotel scrip for Paramount Lodge. So we made a deal. He tore up the rental charge for our cabin. In return, when we were back in the city the next Monday, I searched my files and called a friend or two in order to send Ed photocopies of actual hotel and restaurant scrip being used by other establishments. He then borrowed from this one and that in order to get something that pleased him at Paramount Lodge.

It was only a $75 exchange, but easy for me to fulfill, and it cost Ed nothing but the use of an otherwise vacant cabin. Yet he obtained something he needed, which his own efforts had failed to produce.

A few years ago Gloria Strong, a new member in an organization in which I was quite well known, called me and asked my help. It seemed that she, like many others, wanted to become a writer. Would I give her a little of my time and advice?

I would and did. As it developed, Gloria did not want to be some nebulous kind of writer, but rather a publicity/public relations writer and arranger-of-events.

The result of our conversation was that we made a trade. I agreed to talk with her from time to time, and to coach her in the essentials of the work she aspired to perform. She in turn would type the manuscript of a book I was then writing.

Observing Gloria's personality, and looking at some of her actual written material, I knew that my task would be easy. It was. Within a few weeks Gloria—through my coaching and wire-pulling—had a job as assistant to the advertising manager of a $30-million-a-year manufacturer. And I've never submitted a cleaner script to a publisher.

Of such simple ingredients are satisfying trades created.

Things to Watch for in Heads-Up Trading

- Trading used to be a daily routine of business; now you must make your own opportunities—but trading is essential to business success.

- Trade-club membership can facilitate meeting other traders, but so can getting to know your customers as people.
- Barter exchanges really come down to person-to-person exchanging.
- Dealing face to face minimizes the likelihood of cheating, can enlarge the range of trading between two people, encourages recommending others who will also trade.
- Trading with people who know you is the easy first step.
- Trades may be offered to you on occasion, but you can speed up the exchange process by making the first move yourself.
- When you create the offer, you're free to lay out terms and conditions. The other party is free to reject or alter your proposal, but most often agrees to it as you have stated it.
- Plan your offer, put a little extra value in it (enticement?) *and then make the offer*. The little bit extra is called "boot."
- Boot may be simply words, or may be a tangible added value.
- When you go in person to offer a trade you are more likely to succeed with it than if you telephone.
- Prospect for customers whose businesses are located near those of present customers, by prospecting after finishing up your trip to see one of those current customers.
- Be on the lookout to trade for things besides cash with those you are already selling.
- You should expect to make a good profit, but deliver good service or merchandise in exchange. Otherwise you will hurt your own business and injure the whole trading field in your area.
- Fewer customers and lower prices make for smaller profits, while large volume permits lower prices and still produces profit. Hence the new business entrepreneur very likely must seek goods and situations with extra markup possibilities in order to survive. This changes as business flow increases.

A creative economy is the fuel of magnificence.
—*Emerson*

CHAPTER 8

The Knack of Trading Makes a Creative Retailer

THERE ARE TWIN STRANDS WOVEN TOGETHER in retailing: that of the hunter, who seeks out what he needs where it may be found; and of the farmer, who tills the plot God gave him, let come rain or drought.

In simpler terms: aggressive and passive.

In personalities, these traits may be roughly equated with the *extrovert* and *introvert* which Dr. Jung invented for descriptive clarity.

The roots run deep in American retailing. Aggressive retailers are part of our folklore. Following legend, retailer Jacob Gimbel began his career with a pack on his back, seeking sales by footpath in the back country of early America. Huntington Hartford, who founded the Great Atlantic & Pacific Tea Company, reportedly drove his own tea wagon through the streets of New York searching out customers. Mr. Sears and Mr. Roebuck were aggressive users of advertising space and catalogs, selling by mail to all of the United States, taking quick advantage of the new system of rail transportation and the Post Office's newest service, rural free delivery. This was decades before the U.S. had a highway system or cars to run upon it; and even longer before the development of modern retailing as exemplified by the shopping center at the edge of town.

The aggressive retailers,[1] though, are far outnumbered by the faceless thousands of passive retailers. These are the Smiths, the Joneses, the Johnsons and Williamses of retailing, who in pioneer times established the little crossroads store and then grew up with the town. Throughout our entire mercantile history these good merchants have served their communities well . . . but they have always had their problems *because of* their passivity.

In the early days, it was the catalog sales by mail that hurt their local business. In comparison with the go-getting catalog merchants, they couldn't compete, with either variety of goods or with price.

The next challenge came when the motorcar and our developing network of all-season highways made it possible for the average person to travel to the city to shop for better values or even greater prestige[2] than the hometown merchants provided.

[1] Perhaps I should define "aggressive" as I am using the term. It does not mean offensively pushy or angrily hostile. It merely means actively formulating selling methods and carrying them out by *doing something* to create sales. Originally, aggressive retailers merely took their goods to where their customers were and made it easy for them to buy. Later aggressive retailers used advertising space to bring people in, and consolidated many lines into the "department store" or the "drug store." When ours was a cash economy, aggressive retailers offered to accept credit to make selling easier, and liberal return policies as well as free delivery were other aggressive selling steps. All such developments, historically, were made to the accompaniment of the chorused moans of the majority of passive retailers, who knew their business was being undercut but knew not what to do to counter its effect.

[2] An illustrative instance of this was reported to me by the owner of a large modern furniture store in a county-seat town in the Shenandoah Valley of Virginia. "We carry a lot of standard brands here: Kroehler, Lane chests, Lees and Bigelow carpets—you name it. But all too often one of our customers will come in and shop us, spot the item she wants, then drive nearly three hundred miles round trip to Richmond to make the purchase. When her friends come over to visit she can point to her new furniture or carpet and say, 'Oh, yes, I got it from Miller and Rhoads.' "

Another blow to passive retailers was struck by the growth of chain-store operations. Volume purchasing, mass marketing and modern methods of operation made it possible for these big-time retailers to undercut the small local stores in price while offering greater variety of merchandise and—in some lines—service as well.

Still later, in the years following the Second World War, the burgeoning malls and shopping centers spelled doom to vast numbers of little retail stores that still tried to cling to life in the deserted shells of what once had been bustling, profitable downtown business areas.

The simple techniques of being a passive retailer are easy to tick off:

- Find a community with a high level of spendable income, with enough population to assure patrons, with as little competition as possible.
- Locate your place of business where there's lots of trading traffic, ample parking, and easy access and egress so there's no congestion.
- Stock your shelves with lines the public desires, price your merchandise at a profitable level, make sure your signs and advertising attract potential customers to your store.

Of course there's more to it than that, but not too much. What you've just read (plus charge accounts and perhaps still heavier advertising) makes it possible for both chain stores and franchise stores to open and succeed in thousands of locations across our land.

All of this, as you'll note, is true of retailers trading for *cash*— or for *credit* which at a small discount can be quickly converted to cash. How does it apply to trading for other things?

The aggressive retailer is a *creative* retailer, whether he's trading for cash or for goods. (When he sells, he trades goods for cash;

when he buys, he trades cash for goods . . . so he's in both worlds all the time anyway.)

Mike Romick, who founded Romick's International Tobacco Co., and was the original importer of Douwe Egberts Amphora tobaccos into the United States, started as a retailer in Cleveland. Mike told me once that when he operated his little shop off the lobby of the Hotel Cleveland he made it a practice to ask each customer who bought a pack of cigarettes: "Pardon me, sir, but how long is it since you smoked a pipe?"

This aggressive tactic opened lots of conversations, leading to the sale of many accessories in addition to tobacco, all of which were long-profit items instead of short-profit merchandise which cigarettes are. Mike's aggressive retailing tactics were successful in his own store. Later he applied them in his selling techniques as an importer and distributor, through tens of thousands of retail outlets across the country.

Creativity in retailing means, among other things:

- Being free to explore different ways of buying, selling, displaying, or advertising merchandise.
- Having the openness to the novel so that you are continually testing this, trying that, attempting the other so as to increase volume (and profits).
- Staying alert to special opportunities, even if they lie somewhat outside your regular field.

While these things are true when you are trading for cash, they become even more important when you are trading for other goods or services.

Special Buys for Barter

Be willing to break out of the somewhat narrow mold your aspect of retailing may have placed you in.

As a retailer you have access to the wholesale marketplace. You can, if you choose, buy items at wholesale, and certainly sample lots, far afield from your usual merchandise lines. In many states, where resale licenses are issued to retailers who act as collectors of the state sales taxes, the mere showing of your card or citing your resale license number is sufficient to let you buy almost anything you desire at wholesale prices.

So when you begin to think creatively about trading, goods for goods or goods for services, you can, if you wish, offer much more than just your usual stock in trade.

If you are a retailer handling merchandise where you go to the semiannual market showings, as in ready-to-wear, gifts, furniture, etc., you need merely be on the lookout for special offerings at closeout prices. You can line up any amount of merchandise you may wish that way, either to use as special promotion goods to your cash trade, or as highly tradeable items for barter.

Even if your field has no established market-going habits, still your wholesalers and distributors will make their special deals known through their representatives on their regular calls. Check these out. As you become experienced in barter, you can make it known to your trading partners that special merchandise has become available.

Further, if you follow the trade magazines and listen to the scuttlebutt in your industry, you'll know when a job-lot batch of hardship merchandise is having to be unloaded by some unlucky manufacturer or merchant. If you are an alert retail trader you'll check out such potential profit-makers when they sound interesting, and buy them if you deem it to be correct. Of just such material stuff is success in barter compounded.

In addition to all this, of course, you'll be creatively open to opportunities for trading out your standard merchandise, at regular prices, in exchange for other goods or services you need for your business or personal life. When you make such a trade, for something you'd otherwise have to pay cash to obtain, you have bought the thing you receive at your wholesale cost. You may say, "Well, that's what I do when I use cash—it represents the gross from a sale of an item in which my cost is its wholesale price." Yes, but—the traded exchange is an *extra* sale you would not otherwise have had, on which you pay no sales commission or p.m., and often it is merchandise for which you receive top dollar in barter although not merchantable at that price for cash. Trading is thus more profitable than selling for cash.

In short: use your access to the *cash* marketplace to provide you with trading stock for barter, at better than retail-for-cash profits.

Getting into a Trade Club? Watch Out!

Reread Chapter 3 before seriously committing yourself to a trade-club membership. Make sure you understand all the provisions in the membership application/contract before signing it.

Trade clubs vary in their rules, trading percentages, required limits up to which members must accept trade from other members, and most especially in the character and demeanor of club management and members.

I have known retailers to be "bombed out" by swarming trade-club members in a poorly run club, eager to unload their accumulated credits on the unwary late joiner.

Hank Zuckerman runs a drugstore in a Southern California suburb. He told me that one trade-club husband-and-wife pair came into his store and loaded up shopping carts with more than $700 worth of merchandise and paid for it on trade credits. "Why did you let them?" I asked him. He replied, "The club rules said I had to, and then I didn't know any better."

I could cite similar instances in the case of retail clothiers, beverage retailers, restaurants, florists, jewelers . . . and on and on.

This can happen in a trade club in which the owners have overfloated their trade currency, so that it has become relatively

worthless. Most trade clubs are not this way at all, let me empha-
size. Just to make sure this doesn't happen to you, though, you
can take certain precautionary steps.

- Reread the chapter on trade clubs, and follow the suggestions
  given there about calling up members at random. Do an actual
  survey to get a picture of the state of members' satisfaction, attitude toward how its management functions, and other relevant facts.
- Study the application/contract in detail. Have your lawyer and
  CPA go over it with you if you see fit. Make sure there are no
  hidden liabilities in it which could surprise you unhappily at a
  later date.
- Insist upon whatever qualifications you think are necessary to
  protect you from being overwhelmed with club members' business. These qualifications may involve the use of cash together
  with trade credits. (Cash acts as a damper on trade volume: the
  more cash, the less business.) You may want to say "Percent
  trade negotiable" and leave the matter open for decision on the
  individual merits of each case. Or you may want to say "fifty
  percent cash" to assure you of money for inventory replace-
  ment. Again, after investigation, you may decide that straight
  100 percent trade is quite safe and acceptable. Just make sure
  first.

On this subject, I know a fine local department store in a suburban area near a metropolitan center. The owner became a
trade-club member at 50 percent cash, with the proviso that he
could go to 75 percent cash when his nominal limit of credits had
been reached. He reached the limit cutoff point within a month,
and has been happily trading at the 75/25 ratio ever since.

If the owner had been locked in at 100 percent trade to start, or
even at 50 percent, you can be sure that if still trading at all he
would shortly have been very unhappy. Most likely he would
have been forced to drop out of the club. As it is, members appre-

ciate being able to obtain his fine merchandise at a cash saving of 25 percent.

Setting Up Trading Partners

Any retail establishment buys many things—goods and services—from outside suppliers, not counting inventory itself.

Each of these supply sources, or a substitute source, is a ready-made possibility for opening up a non-cash trading relationship.

I certainly do not advocate ruthlessly throwing out all your cash sources and substituting trade-out suppliers for them. That would be foolish indeed.

Still, if you begin with those suppliers with whom you are not satisfied—because of price, service, merchandise quality, abrasive manners, or anything else—you can gradually supplant them with traders who will supply the same services or materials without cash. These can become just as permanent and satisfactory relationships as if they were predicated on the exchange of cash.

Steven Belden operates a florist shop in a well-heeled suburban community..He's an extremely active trader and a trade-club member, as well as a heads-up trader.

"I have traded for plenty of products as well as services we need," Steve explained. "Before I got into this business I was the vice-president for finances in a major local company. I approach trading the way a controller would approach the money affairs of a business. I am looking for ways to maximize profits.

"When we need something, I think first of trade, then cash if necessary. I see to it that we keep spent down in our trade club, with no great accumulation of credits.

"We have traded for automobile tires and servicing, janitorial supplies, maintenance services, carpentry, painting, electrical work, film processing, and even restaurant accommodations.

"My advice to other retailers who want to trade is, Think of trading *first* when you want to procure something for your business. Use cash only if you can't obtain it through barter."

The extension of Steven's remarks, to make the trading process easier over the long haul, is to make *permanent* trading connections with barterers with whom you strike up a good arrangement.

For a typical retail operation, this might include things such as janitorial services, maintenance, signs and showcards, newspaper or radio advertising, secretarial overload help, accounting or bookkeeping, auto service, tires, printing ... the list could be greatly extended just on business-related requirements. Add to that, if you so decide, another comparable list of personal needs which can also be supplied via barter, and it is easy to see how much of a business's miscellaneous necessities—or those of the owner and family—can be arranged on a regular trade-out basis. These long-term trading partnerships become an easy and profitable way to get what you need at minimum cost in money or effort; on top of that, they build friendships that endure over the months and years. While this may be true in some cases where cash is used, that seldom calls for the personal interchange which is always present in barter.

Trading for—and with—Special Items

If you are a trader in a retail business, keep your eyes open for special opportunities which you can turn to your advantage, even if they are not directly in your particular field of business.

A neighbor of mine, Harry Briggs, runs a paint store. He sells to individual householders, of course, but his principal business is supplying his products in large quantities to painting contractors and apartment-house owners. Harry related this experience to me:

"I went to a wholesale liquidation of paint products, and in addition to the paint I bought I also picked up close to five thousand square yards of foam-backed commercial carpet. This carpet was in several colors, but all that dense, short-pile kind of goods you can walk on forever without wearing it out. Being foam-backed, it didn't need any underlayment. It was in six-foot widths, so any amateur could handle it and lay it.

"I knew that this kind of goods retails regularly at about ten dollars a yard, so when I found I could pick this lot up at one dollar and fifty cents for quick cash, I bought it.

"I let a few of my apartment-house owners know what I had to offer and within a week I had sold two thousand yards of it at four dollars a yard and had my investment back. The bulk of the rest of it I traded to another building owner for a practically brand-new delivery track I needed, and which he pulled away from another business he owned.

"The odd lots I left in stock and have been selling here and there as individual customers want it."

It is easy to see that, on this basis, Harry got a truck free for taking a little risk. Yet it was really a very slight risk; Harry knows his business and his customers' needs very well.

This kind of alert buying—and trading—can be applied in any area of the retail business with equivalent success. You can do it too.

Sometimes opportunity takes the form of an unexpected windfall. In such instances, too, the trader's alertness to values and willingness to step outside normal channels can result in bonanza profits. Here is an instance:

Greg Peters runs an auto-parts store in a small town near me. He revealed that when he was negotiating with the building owner before he took the lease on the premises, he pointed out an accumulation of stuff in the back room.

"Oh, that," the owner said. "My previous tenant had it left over from a restaurant he used to run. He left it and I don't know where to reach him. If it's in your way, call the junk man and have him haul it off."

Greg reported what then happened.

"I took the place, but like most people who open a business, I was short of cash. I couldn't afford to pay to have the place cleaned up and the owner wasn't going to repaint, so while I was doing the work myself I got to thinking about the junk in the back. I looked it over carefully. It turned out to be just about complete stainless-steel equipment for a restaurant kitchen. I almost couldn't believe it.

"I took the owner at his word. I got rid of it—but not to a junk dealer. I worked out a trade with a restaurant supply operator, who has a big line of used equipment. In exchange for the 'junk' in the back room I received cash registers, shelving, and counters I needed for my sales room. It saved me several thousand dollars that I desperately wanted for use elsewhere. That was real luck for me."

Sure, "luck" was involved. But shrewd, worldly old Machiavelli has the appropriate comment in that connection. "Fortune is arbiter of half our actions," said he in *The Prince*, "but she still leaves the control of the other half to us." That's sovereign wisdom.

Keep your attention on affairs related to your business so that you recognize a potential windfall when you see it. Then act on it as daringly/prudently as you judge to be correct. That's the art of the trader applied to the practical affairs of everyday business.

Jane Kirkpatrick operates a successful gift and card shop in a swanky suburb. A divorcee, she is bringing up a daughter now in her teens. Jane gave me the story of how a wise retailer can maximize the use of cash by going outside normal channels to get barter merchandise.

"Janice, my daughter, had to have orthodontics. The dentist gave me a quote for twenty-five hundred dollars—which I didn't have and didn't care to borrow.

"I counteroffered to trade him merchandise which I could obtain for him, instead of cash. It didn't take him long to decide.

"He had been using FM radio-station music in his office, but wasn't pleased with the programming he was getting. What he wanted to do was replace it with stereo tapes off his equipment at home.

"I bought him—at my wholesale—the components for a great quadraphonic system, which he took home. He brought his old gear in and installed it in his office. How he handled his accounting for taxes I don't know and don't care, but I know it cut my outlay for Janice's work just about in half."

Keep your creative thoughts going. You can do likewise.

Now Remember This: Check List of Barter for Retailers

- Retailers come in two types—aggressive and passive.
- The go-getting business owners are not content to wait for customers to come in, they seek them out.
- Aggressive retailing is reflected in all phases of operations, even things as simple as asking a cigarette smoker "Pardon me, sir, but how long is it since you smoked a pipe?"
- Aggressiveness includes alertness to opportunity, openness to try new avenues for profit, willingness to step outside your special field.
- Special buys can add to your profits, whether for cash or barter.
- Trade clubs offer retailers great advantages, but can cause difficulty. Check out a club carefully before signing up; stipulate any necessary protective covenants to prevent your being "bombed out," keep your trade credits spent down, think of "trade first, cash second" when buying miscellaneous things for your business.
- Set up long-term trading partnerships to supply services or goods you use on an ongoing basis.
- Stay awake to special opportunities for trading when unusual circumstances arise.

There are few sorrows, however poignant, in which
a good income is of no avail.   —Logan Pearsall Smith

CHAPTER 9

Trading for the Professional

THIS IS WRITTEN MAINLY FOR THE YOUNG PROFESSIONAL. Those
with well-established practices usually have their income problems pretty well solved by traditional cash patients or clients—
and despite some difficulties with insurance paperwork, credit
clearance and slow pay, are probably content. That, plus the ten-
dency toward orthodoxy in the old, inclines me to believe that
few professionals long in business are going to try a radical "new"
approach to income augmentation such as barter.

Trading, especially as a member of a reliable trade club, may be
an excellent volume builder for the younger doctor, accountant or
lawyer, however.

"If I could totally work out the economics of it, I would prefer
all of my patients to be members of my trade exchange," Henry
Zegzula, a dentist in Federal Way, told me.

Although Henry has been practicing for nearly twenty years,
his reflections on the professional as a trader may express
thoughts of benefit to those less experienced in practice
than he.

"Traders are my kind of people," continued Henry. "They are

largely in business for themselves. They have a similar set of attitudes toward earning a living, about cash flow, credit, taxes, and economics in general. We are more in tune with each other, there's a greater kick in taking care of their needs, and we develop deeper friendships.

"Another thing. When a trader-patient walks in to have work done, I know I'll get paid in full that day. There's no credit problem, no insurance papers to fill out, no time-payment arrangements to make.

"And then traders are usually better fixed financially than the general run of patients. They can afford, and are open to okay, certain procedures which are rarely chosen by most others—such as rebalancing the jaw muscles, for example.

"Since traders can afford the best, they are usually satisfied patients. A happy trader will refer his or her friends, too, which helps build the cash part of my practice.

"I'd say that the young doctor or dentist who has recently opened his office should seriously consider trading as a quick way to build up his practice. Use the trading to obtain many of the things that cash would otherwise have to be used for, leaving the dollars to pay off equipment, to repay education loans, for rent, and all the other things only cash will do for."

Simply extend Dr. Zegzula's remarks to include all the professions, and profit from them in your particular field.

Get Set Before You Start—Analyze Your Costs

The ethics of a particular profession, narrowly construed, might keep some professionals out of trading altogether. They fail to recall what pharmacist Fred Dean told us in Chapter 7: A couple of generations ago, just about all professionals had to trade in order to keep afloat. Such ethics-minded professionals might think nothing of trading in the stock exchanges, or in the commodity market, or for real estate. And they overlook, also, the fact that in any case they are already trading their services for one commodity—money.

Standards in both the dental field and the legal sphere have eased somewhat in recent years; new times are changing many professionals' attitudes toward their own professions and the public's needs. Any strictures still remaining as regards using barter to further a practice will, one hopes, rapidly disappear now that trading is so big and getting bigger by the year.

We'll assume that you as a professional with a practice intend to begin trading where and as feasible. The first thing to do is to analyze your costs.

For example, if you are a dentist or a doctor, you ordinarily make use of laboratory services outside your office. In almost every case you must pay for these services in cash; and some of them run into high dollar figures.

If you plan to trade, look these items over. Can you afford to *include* these costs as part of your barter, or must you recover costs?

Or say you are a lawyer. You may have to pay someone else for research, or for typing documents, or for taking depositions and transcribing them. Then there are messenger costs . . . and so on. How much of this can you afford to absorb in your trading? Will you have to make some or all of such costs *cash* items outside your barter arrangements?

Perhaps accounting is your profession. Will you look for cash as an extra item when you trade your services, to cover outlays for computer time, for instance?

Or again, as an architect or engineer, you may or may not wish to include more than your own conference time and rough sketches or preliminary analyses in your trading. You may feel that the costs to include a full set of plans, or a detailed set of figures, will require more outlay than you can absorb without some cash back.

Be Sure You Get Your Cash Back

If you are operating close to the margin in your practice, it may be a business necessity to trade only when you can stipulate that "out-of-pocket cash costs are payable in cash" and make that an up-front part of all barter deals.

If you do make such a requirement, you will find that you do somewhat less volume in trading than if you were willing to absorb all such costs and trade even-Steven with your clients or patients. Also, you are likely to find that the cash gained will be offset by the cash your trading partners now likewise demand for *their* outlays in money.

However, much depends upon your own attitude. You may very well obtain all the trading volume you desire while still getting your cash back for necessary outlays. And you may even do this while not paying the equivalent cash to those you are bartering with.

Professionals are the favored few, in that they have won through to their licensed positions in the world as the result of long schooling and training, during which time they absorbed also much of the *spirit* of their profession. This esprit engenders a confidence that enables them to deal with others from a position of authority and eminence, and also allows them to set up better trading postures than those without such a background.

So you can really make your own mind up. If you feel you need the cash, you can probably get it. To ask for cash may, however, cut down on your trading volume. It is sure to take some of the sheer fun out of bartering. But *economically* you will no doubt come out ahead.

Allocate Your Trade Time—Fill Up Your Slow Days

No trading CPA of my acquaintance would think of taking on a new barter client from January 1 to April 15 of any year. If you are a public accountant you too will wish to accept barter clients only during the relative lull of summer and fall. (Unless you are like Sib Hansen, Los Angeles CPA, who from his earliest years made it a rule to set up his clients' fiscal years to end at staggered intervals around the calendar, so as to avoid sleepless nights of work at certain periods.)

So too whatever your profession. Look at your daybook. Note which days of the week, hours of the day, or times of month or year give you the most unbooked time. Fit your trading clientele or patients into those periods, to the extent you can.

Dr. Tom Kutrosky, of North Hollywood, long-time trader, told me he plans to schedule most barter patients in on Thursdays, an off day for his other patients.

The whole idea, as you can see, is to fill out your schedule with trader-patients or barter-clients, not to overwork yourself or your assistants during periods when you are already busy.

You're in charge. Plan your trading to your own maximum convenience as well as benefit.

The Plus and Minus of Joining a Trade Club

Reread the analysis of trade clubs in Chapter 3 before making up your mind whether to join a club or not.

Note these factors which may incline you *to* take out a membership in a club in your community:

- Trade clubs just about guarantee to bring you extra clientele or patients. Medical doctors, dentists, optometrists, CPAs, architects, and many other specialists rate high on the demand list by club members.

- If you don't wish to be listed in a directory as a trader, for professional-ethics reasons, arrange for the club office to give out your name to other members only on inquiry.
- Just about all the time-consuming negotiating and bird-dogging are removed from trading when you deal with other members. That's a great time saver if you are fairly busy, and find it difficult to get out of your office for extended periods.
- Your high hourly rates, or fees for various procedures, just about assure that you will be in a favorable position vis-à-vis other club members. Trade-club credits are easier to get than dollars, so you will be able to obtain plenty for your needs without overburdening your schedule with barter folk.

Offsetting these plus factors:

- When you join a trade club you may have to agree to absorb more barter business than you really want before you reach your cutoff point. (At least it may seem like a lot of volume to begin with.)
- Then too, you have a cash outlay to join a club, and more cash on a continuing basis (in fees or annual renewals) as long as you are a member. While the fees are modest, they still are a continual drain on the otherwise 100-percent benefits of direct barter outside a club.
- Also, if you are somewhat inexperienced in trading, you may get frustrated because not everything you need or desire is readily available within the membership of your trade club. This may be merely a mild frustration, but I have observed it occasionally as a real aggravation which led to a turn-off about trading in general.

I'd say that the professional who really wants to take the little trouble required can gain far more from a trade club than he is likely to lose. But here again, make your own determination based on your practice, your profession, the community in which you locate, and the club or clubs available to you there.

Trading as an Aid to Investing

This book is not written for the fully experienced traders of this world, of whom the professions certainly have their fair share. There are many doctors, lawyers, accountants, and others who already have far more experience than you or I in the field of real estate trading, commodities, stocks and bonds, and so on.

There is no easier way to become an expert in trading in general, though, than through making it part of your normal day-to-day routine. Someone who has dealt with the down-to-earth realities of trading on a small scale, and has learned the principles involved, will be in a good position to minimize risks and maximize gains when large-scale trading comes along.

Even as a beginning trader, especially as a trade-club member, you will find investment opportunities opening up. Read the whole of Chapter 12 for ways to use barter for real estate investing—a special subject in itself.

Other openings abound, both direct and indirect.

Maurice Hart, an attorney-at-law in Century City, some time ago set up a general-limited partnership deal for a corporate client. He walked away with a share for himself as compensation—a direct investment that paid regular dividends and appreciated in value as time went by.

Sib Hansen, CPA, already mentioned, once took 10 percent of a client's company in exchange for his continuing services over a period of time. That's another direct investment.

Harry Gorton, a specialist writer of promotional materials, was able to negotiate minor cash compensation but a percentage of equity in a new publication, for which he provided a complete promotional package to kick off its introductory advertising and subscription programs. (The magazine became a great success, to Harry's vast satisfaction.) That was still another direct investment.

Trade-club credits can be used for investment purposes, too. I know several steady customers in trade clubs who buy good original paintings and ceramics with trade credits. They enjoy their possessions while watching them appreciate in value in the *cash* marketplace.

Indirectly, trading has an even broader part to play for the investment-minded professional.

The realities of a professional practice are that the bulk of what a young person earns are the result of his or her direct personal efforts. If the earnings are ever to exceed what personal services can supply, they must come through investment in profit-producing ventures. This may be done directly, as we have seen, with barter as the medium. More likely, it will require *cash* to fuel the investment engine effectively.

Being able to set aside cash for investment on a continuing schedule can be arranged quite easily *if* the professional obtains many of the usual necessities of business and personal life via trading, in addition to the normal cash income from regular practice.

Thus barter *offsets* a sizeable amount of cash outlay in the budget, freeing that amount for other uses, including investment.

The mathematics are simple. Trading circles among business and professional people I know estimate that a good mix includes about 15 to 20 percent barter *in addition* to the normal volume for cash. If a substantial portion of the cash thus loosened from day-to-day requirements is devoted to well-chosen investments, it is easy to see that later-life security is practically assured and with no great strain.

This is a matter for each professional to think through for himself, in conjunction with legal and tax advisers. Yet its importance for long-term success can scarcely be overemphasized.

Highlights of Trading for the Professional

- Trading can help build volume for the young practitioner.
- Barter clientele brings the professional exciting contacts with other business people, who share similar views and problems.
- There are no collection problems with trader-patients or clients, and they spend freely.
- Traders can afford the best, they tend to be happy clients, they recommend friends who become cash customers.
- Young professionals who trade for many business or personal necessities make more cash available to pay off equipment, educational loans, and the like.
- Before trading, analyze your costs.
- If you judge it to be necessary, require cash in addition to trade so as to compensate you for supplies or services you must pay cash to obtain for your barter clients.
- Arrange your trade business so that it does not interfere with your cash patronage, and so that you will fill up empty spots in your calendar rather than overload yourself at busy times.
- A trade club membership practically assures you of added patients or clients. On the whole, there may be more advantages than disadvantages for you in becoming a trade-club member.
- Trade-club or direct-barter activities, if allowed to fill up an additional 15 to 20 percent of your schedule, can provide the wherewithal for direct investment or, by offsetting cash outlays you would otherwise have to make, free the equivalent dollar amounts for investing.

You pay a great deal too dear for what's given freely.
—Shakespeare

CHAPTER 10

How to Trade if You Are into Crafts or Provide a Service

IN THE GENERAL RUN OF RETAIL LINES, in which merchants handle standard lines of products, pricing is not so much a matter of individual choice as it is for the skilled craftsman, artist, or service person.

The wholesale market price is much the same for all retailers who buy from their established sources. Business costs require an additional markup; and the profit is added on top of that. Still, the big store and the small shop will be at most a few cents apart on the dollar as far as their selling prices are concerned.

Notice that this is for *standard* lines of merchandise.

Skilled-trades people and service specialists are likewise governed to some degree by the marketplace and its going rates in the locality in which such people are operating. Still, there is great latitude in pricing these somewhat standard services too. If you have ever asked for bids on a remodeling job, or for building a new room on your house, you will know from personal experience that there can be a wide range of pricing services based on the identical specifications.

In the area of creative crafts and the various art spheres, the spread of pricing is much wider still. You can buy a three-by-four-foot painting for your living room, framed and ready to hang, for as little as fifteen or twenty dollars. You *can* spend that many thousands of dollars . . . or hundreds of thousands.

If you are intending to sell—or barter—how you go about it has a great deal to do with which end of the value scale you will be trading at.

Positive Ways of Pricing Your Products

The first thing to recognize is that, as an independent trader, even if you are doing the work yourself, when you sell to the general public (or barter with it) you must deal at *retail* prices.

If you have been selling through stores or galleries, they have marked up what they have paid you. Such markups vary with the situation and the artist, but I know of instances in which the gallery buys at 25¢ and sells at 100¢ on the dollar. A 50 percent gross margin for the retailer is common: that's the percentage most usual in gift lines of merchandise.

It is important for you to price your merchandise accordingly.

Similarly if you are skilled in one of the trades, or are an expert in servicing or repairing equipment: as an independent trader you must quote your jobs at contractors' prices. This will be quite a bit more than the hourly rates *paid* by contractors for the sort of work you are performing.

A Standard Price List Is the Creative Way to Go

William Brooks is a highly successful Seattle artist, who sells through galleries and has had many one-man shows. Each of his works is recorded in his master inventory list, priced, and photo-recorded; and notations are made as to where and when the piece has been shown. When Bill trades a picture, as he occasionally does, there is no question as to what it should be worth. His methods are typical of artists of established reputation.

Dennis Svoboda is a highly skilled craftsman in wood. He makes distinctive frames for the etched mirrors which he and his partner create and market. For some years they sold their merchandise mostly from mall showings. As they found that certain designs were more popular than others, they standardized them into lines that simplified both production and pricing. At this point, having grown large enough in their craft business to be able to seek regular distribution, they have developed catalog sheets and price lists to simplify ordering and pricing procedures all down the line to the public. Yet even at the beginning they set a good value on their products.

"Believe me, trading has been our salvation," Dennis told me. "Especially in our early days, I'd look first for what I wanted in terms of who I could trade with. Having our things priced right was essential."

Harold Garner is a journeyman plumber in Southern California. Even in that land of perpetual sun there are days when he does not work on a regular construction job; and he also has weekends and evenings free. Harold markets his services very easily through membership in a trade club.

"I make a good living from my regular work," Harold told me. "After all, hourly rates are pretty high. But my wife and I like some of the fringes and luxuries too, and that's what I provide for us by moonlighting for trade credits. I charge myself out just the way a contractor would, and have no trouble getting my prices from other club members. I can afford the moderate transaction fees because I have a good profit spread. Then I convert my credits into resort or travel accommodations.

"We took a trip to Hong Kong that way last year, and had a ball. I used trade units for rental on a motor home a couple of years back. We loved it, so I traded my services as the down payment on one of our own.

"Trading is really the way to go, but it works better if you put a good value on your services. You are well compensated for the bother of working with trade credits or setting up other barter deals. Your customer gets better service than if he'd called in a contractor, because you give him personal attention. It's a good deal all around."

Lisa Casey was a very shy, tense young woman when I first met her. (She came at the suggestion of a mutual friend, to get my advice on wording an announcement she wanted to have printed.) For several years she had been "throwing pots" and yet had never sold or exhibited any of them. Her garage was apparently filled to bursting with ceramics of varying degrees of attractiveness, reflecting her learning experience in that difficult craft.

At my suggestion, she exhibited at an arts and crafts show sponsored by an organization in which we were both members. She put very modest prices on her wares, in my view (although they were nearly astronomical figures to her) and actually sold more than $200 worth for cash. In addition, several other exhibitors sought her out and initiated trades with her for their merchandise, to their mutual satisfaction.

"I wouldn't have thought it possible that people would pay those prices for my work," Lisa said afterward. "What amazed me even more was that those other craftsmen and artists, who ought to know better, wanted my things badly enough to talk up a trade for them.

"What an education this has been for me."

Previously, Lisa had never sold or traded anything—because she thought so little of her work she would not show it or price it. When she gave in to my "strongarm" tactics, and did show it, she was amazed. A year or so later she was a regular exhibitor at every fair she could get to. Needless to say, her prices kept going up. She graded her pots, and set prices by the grade, which made convenient stepups (or stepdowns) for the buying public or traders she dealt with.

How to Be Sure You Get Your Cash Back

It isn't always important to have cash involved in a trade. Whether you do or not will depend upon many factors, which you must determine for yourself.

Still, if you decide you *must* have cash as part of the deal, here are two stratagems which will prove useful to you in negotiating that into your arrangement.

First, as a craftsman or tradesman you are certainly entitled to receive cash for out-of-pocket expenses for materials, rental of needed special equipment, and perhaps even mileage or extra payment for use of your truck, etc. Merely include these items in your proposal—or your response to some other person's offer—and you will have little trouble collecting for them. It's usual for the person charging for such items to keep receipted bills of everything purchased, and to log time or miles in a daybook or other record, for settling at the end of the project.

Second, some kinds of art projects can involve cash expenditures you are justified in recovering. If you paint a mural, and have to rent scaffolding as well as supply paint by the gallon, you can include cash for these things in your initial agreement. You may have only a few dollars in paints, stretcher, and canvas, but you might well require cash for the seventy-dollar frame around the painting you are trading for several hundred dollars. One man I met wanted to trade at 100 percent—except, he said, he was represented by an agent and needed 10 percent cash for him! (We did not get together.)

Ways of Promoting Yourself to Other Traders

First thing is to find the other traders. You can do this by dropping in to see people who have the thing or service you want, and offer to swap what you have directly with them. If they are willing to trade, but don't need your product or service, you may be able to trade your thing to a third party who will give you what the second person wants. Three-legged trades are not at all uncommon.

Next to going directly after what you want, advertising your craft products, skills, or services to members of a trade club is the easiest method of flushing the live traders out of the bushes. Even if you are not a trade-club member, if you can borrow a friend's directory, you can set up contacts which will lead to trades. Since directories are categorized for the convenience of members, it's easy enough to spot people in the field you're concerned about who are also known traders.

If you are a member of a trade club, of course, you can utilize the office's services in steering you to where you can get what you want. Or if vending your products or services is uppermost in your mind, the club will possibly let you take space in its directory to advertise. It even might permit you to supply a quantity of a circular you have had printed, and include a copy in each statement it mails out to members some month.

Another very easy and reliable method of locating traders is to advertise your offer and wants in your local classified section or on neighborhood bulletin boards. Once you get replies, use your price list, descriptive circular, or anything else needed, to effect the barter transaction on good terms for both parties.

By attending art fairs you will rub easels with other art types, many of whom trade, and with whom you'll find it easy to set up deals. More general fairs, with exhibitors from many fields, will accomplish a similar end on a broader scale of merchandise and services.

Writing a barter column for your local paper spreads the word about your interests. Try it!

Let's Go over That Once More

- As a craftsman, artist, tradesman, or service specialist, you have considerable leeway in setting your price structure.
- Be sure you price your products or services to trading partners at their retail level, not the wholesale price you'd accept from an employer or a distributor or dealer.
- Standardize your prices and record your inventory, if you are an artist, or list your services, if you are a technical or craft expert.
- If your business expands so that you wish to seek regular distributors, you will want to develop catalog sheets also. (Even then, if you're trading, do it at the suggested retail price, not the wholesale figure.)
- If you decide you need cash as part of a trade, base it on realities such as materials, equipment rental, mileage, or other factors, which you then document with receipts and settle for at the end of the project.
- You can find other traders, and promote yourself to them, by personal contact, phone and mail solicitation, and by following up leads found in trade-club directories. If you belong to such a club get its office personnel to help locate what you want (buying or selling) and advertise in the club's directory. Local classified ads, neighborhood weeklies, and notices posted on bulletin boards can all produce trading action, as can contacts made with fellow exhibitors at fairs.

It is naught, it is naught, sayeth the buyer: but when he is gone his way, then he boasteth.

—Proverbs 20:14

CHAPTER 11

Close-Up View of Due-Bills,
Scrip, and Brokers

A DUE-BILL IS A BRIEF WRITTEN ACKNOWLEDGMENT of a debt, but is not payable to order. Some companies use them to keep records of employees' "draws" between paydays. Banks occasionally use them instead of cashiers' checks. The resort, hotel, and travel industry utilizes them extensively, especially in exchange for advertising time and space.

A bit of historical background may help put due-bills in their true perspective.

In the decades which followed the extension of railroads to both coasts, and from the Great Lakes and New England to the Gulf, travel in the United States became possible on a broader scale than previously.

Transportation companies fostered travel, and the development of business and industry along their routes. Railroads in particular ran excursions, sometimes at merely token amounts, for hundreds or even thousands of miles, in order to stimulate population growth and economic activity in system cities and towns.

Hotels and resorts sprang up, catering to the new traveling public. The railroads and, to a lesser extent, the steamship carriers, were the only practical means of transportation open to the traveler who wanted to reach those hostelries and watering places. There were no national highways. The motorcar had not yet been developed.

Trade and barter were generally recognized as standard business methods in those years. Cash was in shorter supply than it is now. There was no national credit system such as that which we take for granted. Result: hotel and resort owners bartered accommodations for advertising space in newspapers and magazines. The documents used were due-bills, a term still in vogue today.

Over the intervening decades the due-bill market has risen and fallen with the tides of the general economy.

During the two big wars, due-bills practically disappeared from the scene. Everyone had cash; no one had accommodations. In depressed times, or during periods when competition has been heavy, due-bills flourish. In recent years there has been a luxuriant new growth of these markers, along with restaurant scrip and charter-travel and cruise paper.

Just What Is a Due-Bill?

We're using "due-bill" as a general term to designate any written agreement by a hotel, motel or resort to provide a given dollar amount of accommodations (with or without food or beverages, clubhouse privileges, etc.) under conditions stated in the document itself.

Metropolitan newspapers, national magazines, radio and TV stations, outdoor advertising companies and other media can obtain all the due-bills they care to use in exchange for advertising in their media.

Some of them can and do use such due-bills as a special kind of currency, which they trade for other commodities. Much of the due-bill volume funnels through the hands of a number of large-scale due-bill brokers.

An important point to remember about due-bills is this: cash is a "harder" (stronger) commodity than due-bills. (The hotel or resort people would have sold the accommodation for cash if they could have done so.) Therefore, due-bills are generally available on the *cash* marketplace at a discount from regular posted prices.

Discount Scales to Be Aware of

The "softness" of any particular hotel's due-bill (or the paper of any cruise company, motel chain, restaurant, resort, etc.) depends on the degree of distress present in the particular management's situation.[1] Because of this, there are no standard discounts in the

[1] Any commodity that is time-sensitive can become a "distress" item and thus find a sale in the marketplace only at a reduced price. The degree of distress potential for each commodity group varies with its exposure to deterioration or disappearance as time passes.

Day-old bread, for instance, sells at a small discount. For most real purposes it is as good as it was the day before. Last season's styles of ready-to-wear can usually be moved at discounts in the 10- to 30-percent range. (Still older style-oriented items may require more drastic price cuts in order to be cleared out.)

However, there is another kind of commodity which is 100 percent discounted in a single day—and which leaves no remains at all. This is the *personal time* of professional and service people, the *air time* of television and radio stations, the *unfilled ad space* in a given edition of a newspaper or magazine, and the *empty room or cabin* of a hotel/motel or cruise ship, or *vacant seat* on an aircraft. Federal law prohibits air carriers in the United States from bartering accommodations, although no such prohibition exists on charter flights to overseas destinations or on foreign carriers' overseas routes. Nor does any law forbid media or profesionals or the travel/hotel industry from moving empty time or accommodations at whatever rates they find necessary.

If you operated a broadcast facility, you'd already know that a sharp buyer late on Friday afternoon can buy your unsold weekend availabilities at a fraction of what the normal buyer pays. The philosophy is, Better get a little something than have the unsold time disappear forever without any return whatever.

Other media have the same motivations to a lesser degree, since they have manufacturing costs to consider. Still a smart negotiator can frequently cut magazine costs to a fraction of rate-card scales by bargaining for the odd remainder space left in some regional sections of national magazines.

With professionals and service people, trading for other goods or services

due-bill field. If you are an individual buyer, looking for a week's cruise for yourself and spouse, you might expect to get a discount of 15 to 25 percent, depending on circumstances. Anything less would scarcely be worth your while in seeking out a broker and negotiating a deal. But if you are a corporate buyer, looking for resort accommodations for a company meeting of 150 executives and their wives, your cash could conceiveably command an even better discount.[2] Your trading skills become important here in

---

[2] The due-bill brokerage business is clandestine, so don't look for ads in any publication offering discounted media availabilities, cruise-ship accommodations or hotel/resort rooms.

All such negotiations are kept under cover out of necessity to protect the existing publicly posted rate structures of the operators involved.

A cruise operator, for instance, would find it difficult or impossible to placate the travel agents throughout the world if its policy of discounting accommodations became public knowledge. (Travel agents operate on discounts of 7 to 10 percent for most carriers; you can imagine their reaction if it were widely proclaimed that the man in the street—their own potential customer—was able to buy through other sources at far under their own buying figure.) Who would pay retail if he could with little effort find a way to buy at below wholesale?

Exactly the same situation exists with respect to media rates, professional fees, and the going charges for hotel and resort rooms. In order to protect the higher publicly announced rates, deals for less money or in exchange for other things are kept from public view.

The brokers involved do a great deal of self-policing in order to protect their carrier or hotel clients (and just incidentally, to safeguard the good thing they themselves have going). For instance, if you have been booking a cruise or tour

---

usually takes the place of actual rate cutting.

If you have a cruise sailing at a certain date, or have massive unbooked hotel/resort accommodations at an upcoming season, you are faced with the necessity of doing something. You have already prodded your agents and their best has left you with masses of unsold space. If the ship sails without its full complement of passengers (or the night passes with the hotel rooms empty) you have lost forever your chance to sell the space. Yet if you can recover even a fraction of that unbooked potential, you will help your overall operations by that much.

Motivations such as these, which differ from company to company, season to season and even day to day, are what produce a thriving discount market in due-bills, cruise accommodations, and advertising time/space.

negotiating the best price for the most complete package you can arrange.

Locating Sources of Scrip and Due-Bills

If you are merely interested in getting a cruise, hotel or resort accommodations, or restaurant scrip for your personal use, it is simplest to check out one of the sources listed in Appendix 2. For the amount you plan to spend, there would be little advantage in doing a great deal of shopping around, and you could waste a lot of time.

---

through the same travel agent every year for the past while, you may find a due-bill or travel-paper broker unwilling to sell to you at discount. He will fear repercussions if and when the agent you previously dealt with finds out and complains to the carrier or hotel management. Likewise, if you have been arranging conventions for your company and using the retail-level rate structure, the broker might decline to book your 150-person package at discounted rates lest his principals at the hotel or resort cut him out of their marketing system entirely when they find out.

The same general situation exists with regard to radio, TV, magazine, and other media rates. Although barter exists in the advertising world, to the tune of hundreds of millions of dollars per year, it is all arranged quietly. Many advertising agents, operating their own media-buying departments for years, may never have become involved in that aspect of the business at all.

In each case, to make sure you can barter (or buy at substantial discount), observe these points:

- Be able to demonstrate that your business is *plus* business, not just regular cash business switched to discount, or shifted to barter.
- Be willing to play the game as professionals do—keep it quiet, don't boast to your friends, don't discuss details with fellow guests.
- Be sure you can make decisions and abide by them. You are buying *distress* merchandise. You should no more think of being a no-show and wanting your money back than you would expect to return merchandise bought at a year-end clearance in a department store.
- Cash talks. Don't try to play credit-card games, don't ask for extended terms, don't try to get the broker to hold while you discuss terms or conditions with your spouse or associates.

If you are planning a meeting or group outing or convention for your organization, though, you might profitably spend some time investigating discount deals for cash or even some kind of barter plan to provide the services you need. When your budget begins to reach the multiple thousands of dollars range, you become of interest to bigger operators and your negotiating strength increases accordingly.[3]

If you are an experienced and hard-nosed bargainer, the simplest course is to approach the establishment or carrier obliquely, avoiding the general sales staff completely. Find out whether they have another separate office which handles barter deals (many of the fanciest do). You may have, or can obtain at discount for

[3] A full discussion of corporate barter is outside the scope of this book. You may wish to explore its potentials if you own or are an executive of a manufacturing company, major service business, or advertising medium. A number of advertising-related trade brokers, who stock inventories of goods taken in barter deals as well as provide inventories of advertising, cruises, rooms, and restaurant services, are ready to discuss trading your products/services for what they have. You must be able to deliver what you promise, and you should know what you want, but if what you offer is a sound value you should be able to swap advantageously. You will usually have to pay a broker's commission in cash (15 percent is typical, but you can negotiate a better deal if you are strong enough). Often a company can enhance its appearance on its annual report by being able to show under its list of assets a prepaid advertising budget of thousands or hundreds of thousands of dollars. This can be arranged by swapping its *hard* products at their inventory valuation for relatively *soft* radio, TV, magazine, or newspaper advertising time and space. Like magic, an asset has doubled in value (to all appearances) and a product, dull in itself, has been used as the value which will buy a massive promotion campaign that will make it an exciting sales success. On another level, a political campaign manager who also knows the barter business can take a few thousands of dollars worth of cash contributions and convert them to hard goods at discount (cars or car leases, television sets, etc.) and then parlay these into two or three times the dollar value in air time. If you are interested in exploring such possibilities for your company, sift through a few trade brokers until you find one you can work with intelligently. Learn from him on enough deals so you have the basics well in hand. Then go after trade deals on your own. Appendix 2 lists names you may find useful as a starter.

cash, items or services the organization needs. By a bit of extra work you might make your dollars go twice as far as they would have if you had gone in the front door.

If you are large enough as a manufacturer or service organization, you may cut things to bedrock by bartering a quantity of your products or services for what you need, dealing with one of the brokers specializing in corporate barter negotiations. He will be accustomed to setting up three-party trades, or may be able to supply out of his own inventory what the party wants who will deliver what you need. Reciprocal traders develop huge inventories of their own by taking goods/scrip in payment or part payment of their commissions. Here you are dealing with Party A, who has what you desire, and a reciprocal trader who has what Party A wants (or can get it for him). All you have to do is supply the reciprocal trader with what *he* wants in order to get the deal put together.

And certainly there is nothing against your doing the entire job yourself, if you have the personality and the turn of mind necessary for top-flight barter. That way you don't have any brokerage fees to pay, do not need to rely upon the performance of middlemen, and can generally sharpen your advantages.

Due-Bill Brokers—The Pros and Their Cons

You need have no fear in dealing with the larger, well established due-bill and scrip brokers. Their business prospers largely by satisfied customers coming back again, and letting their friends in on a good thing. It is a matter of business policy for them to deliver exactly what they say they will do, without hiding flaws from their customers.

Every field of commerce has its shadier element; due-bills are no exception. A few points to watch out for when dealing with the smaller operators in the business (and even with some of the shakier and flakier principals) include these:

- There is a short time-limit on the scrip or due-bill, so that in order to use it you have to go right now. (Be sure that your restaurant or hotel paper has at a minimum a good long life; preferably it should be good until used.)
- There is a cash surcharge or service fee which must be paid along with the scrip or due-bill. (Watch this. Sales taxes, gratuities, and other services such as telephone, laundry, greens fees, and so on, are just about always separate items which you must pay in cash. Fair enough. But the operators may want some additional cash as a "service fee." If the added cash amounts to any appreciable percentage, it will be the institution's way of recovering some of its own costs, hence will not be as fair a trade deal for you.)
- If you are a trade-club member, you may be offered hotel-motel-resort due-bills at half cash and half trade credits. This is no great bargain. If you can get the accommodations for 100 percent trade credits, fine. Not so if you must pay cash too. Your broker has acquired it for all trade, and is cashing out at your expense. If you simply go to a due-bill broker with an all-cash offer, you may be able to get an equivalent set of accommodations for the same or a bit more cash as you would have spent on the fifty-fifty deal within your trade club. You will have saved your trade credits.
- Keep your eyes peeled for switching of prices. You may think you have booked an accommodation at a given rate, only to find on arrival at the resort/hotel/motel that the only availabilities are at a larger cost. You must come up with the difference in cash. Make sure of rates before you go.
- Pin down details about included services. If you *think* you are entitled to room, food and beverages, greens fees, health club, and so on but discover after arrival that all these items are cash

add-ons, you'll be chagrined and angry. Again, be certain before you sign up the deal that all the items you *think* are in the package really *are* there.

If you are dealing with a reputable broker, and his client hotel or resort operator comes on with any of these sly tricks, let him know what happened. He will straighten it out with the operator or executive responsible and will thank you for it.

Trade Brokers and How to Use Them

There is no big secret in using a trade broker—it's just like employing a special agent in a profession or service industry. However, since there are no policing agencies within the field, and no licensing requirements in order to set up shop as a trade broker, you will want to make your own evaluation on the basis of the broker's qualifications. He will be involved in transferring thousands of dollars of your company's assets to third parties. You will be relying upon him to obtain in return what you have specified you want in the way of merchandise, materials, or services.

Check out your broker every way that seems reasonable. Run a credit rating on him, if that seems feasible. Check references, in the form of satisfied clients, if you can get him to give you such contacts.

There is one thing to remember, though—and to make allowances for. A good trade broker is pure *entrepreneur*. He has what Pareto called "the instinct for combinations." He operates on the exchange spectrum at different places than do ordinary businessmen.

As a result, he will display many of the characteristics which drive company controllers (and others with equally conservative instincts) up the wall.

The trade broker will usually depend more on what he has in

his head than what he has in the bank. Although he may honor written contracts, and even insist upon them, he is also willing to operate on oral commitments from those he trusts. Instead of going the "normal" direct way, paying the asking price in cash, he takes indirect routes to his goals. This indirectness may appear to be deviousness; in any case it is outside the bounds of usual business practice, and arouses the suspicions of those whose experience has been confined to the better-known pathways of commerce.

Then too, a good trade broker is usually quite frank and direct in manner, despite the obliqueness of his trading angle. He frequently brushes aside initial "no" answers. He breaks out of the usual lines of company hierarchy and goes directly to the top. He tends to talk in big figures, and to offer the potential of large profits.

If you can quiet your own conservative instincts enough to listen, evaluate, and decide on a realistic basis (not just from your bias of doubt that such a personality type arouses), you may have a jewel to cherish.

A good broker *can* help you make enormously profitable transactions. He *can* do things without cash, or with little cash, which the general run of business executives find quite incredible. He is justified in speaking in large numbers, because he is used to dealing with them.

If you pay him his fee in cash, he will have earned it.

If you seek to accomplish the same ends *without* him, you will discover that you yourself must think and act in exactly the same ways in order to get the same work done. It is usually simpler to pick up a seasoned broker to do the work for you.

We'll assume that you have checked out one or two brokers and have located one with whom you'd like to try a transaction or two.

First step is a discussion with him. It will involve what you have to trade—its nature and dollar amount—and what you desire in return. You will get an indication from your broker as to how quickly and well he can work out the details of the transaction. (He may be able to match your requirement at once from other clients' offerings; he may have to search for what you want.) You will also pin him down as to fees. These are negotiable, like everything else. He will ask for cash. You may, if you desire, counter-offer a greater value in your merchandise and/or service.

Many trade brokers began as advertising agency operators. They like to think that 15 percent is an industry standard for their commission. It isn't. Even in the advertising agency business proper, there's a lot of rebating and commission-cutting going on. Feel free to negotiate the best deal you can, commensurate with the value of the service performed. In general, the greater the dollar amount involved, the less the percentage you should pay as a fee.

You may have "hard" goods to offer—appliances, cars, audio equipment, cameras, and so on. In such case, you are in a better position to get *more* than just the dollar equivalent in media space and time or routine services. Make sure your broker understands that you know this.

If you have "soft" items to trade, be willing to add more into the deal to work it out *if necessary.* But don't start out that way. And make certain your broker knows that you understand that too.

After all, unsophisticated types in businesses all over the land buy "soft" and "hard" commodities and services every day at full retail prices, and for cash. Therefore, any strength or weakness in what you are trading or trading for gets important only as you negotiate for it. Make sure that you and your broker see eye to eye on this, so that you don't settle for less than you might easily get, just so he can put together a transaction with greater ease.

You will no doubt want your broker to work quietly, so as not to disturb your regular business channels. You may even wish to provide him with a list of people *not* to contact, or company policies which must not be infringed upon.

Finally, you will convert everything to writing. Probably your broker has a standard listing form, much like a real estate broker or business-opportunity specialist. Even so, this is subject to reworking if you decide it is necessary—especially his "standard" fees, which will no doubt be printed as part of the form. If necessary, have your legal counsel draw up an appropriate form, or at least check over the one you propose to sign. When all signals are green, sign the papers and turn the broker loose.

You may get negligible results. Or you may find that, lo! for a relatively small fee you can turn enormous profits, on paper or actual or both. There's one thing you can be sure of. You will receive the beginnings of an education in aspects of the business world that are hidden from most executives. Some of the broker's entrepreneurial genius may even rub off on you, to your lasting benefit.

Let's Replay That Record

- A due-bill is a brief acknowledgment of a debt; but as used in these pages it also means letters of credit, scrip issued by a company payable in goods or services, or other paper which can be converted in a similar fashion.
- Due-bills are frequently generated when hotel/resort/cruise operators use them to pay for advertising space in newspapers and magazines; they are also used to purchase other goods and services.
- Due-bills are available on the cash marketplace at substantial discounts from face value.
- Due-bills are time-sensitive, since an accommodation not occupied on a given day represents a value lost beyond recovery;

hence whatever it can be sold for is a gain. (The same applies to radio-TV time and, to a lesser degree, to magazine and newspaper space.)

- Due-bills are bought and sold in a gray-market area of business. The issuers of such paper sell it on the quiet so as to recover what they can without upsetting the market for their product at its full public rate.
- Be prepared to play the game when you negotiate for scrip or due-bills with a broker. Make a decision and stick to it. Don't boast to outsiders about your bargain purchase. Don't try to renege.
- Keep your eyes open for possible negative factors in the paper you're buying. Avoid short cutoff dates. Make sure of accommodation rates. Verify exactly what extras are included. Be certain there won't be added cash surcharges.
- You may want to use a trade broker to swap quantities of your product or service for other things you need. If so, check out his bona fides as well as you can, making allowances for his quite different operating methods.
- If you want to accomplish a trade broker's task yourself, you will find yourself operating in much the same way he does— quite a bit out of the ordinary conservative path of usual business practices.

Help, Hands, for I have no lands.
—*Benjamin Franklin*

CHAPTER 12

The Place of Barter in Real Estate

MOST OF US NEVER GET INTO TRANSACTIONS bulking larger in dollar amounts than our real estate purchases and sales. No matter how frugal or clever, few of us accumulate all the cash we need to go into a real estate purchase with all the "down" required. If we are buying, we'd therefore do well to seek alternatives to money in order to get into the property we want. If we are selling, we can ease our problem of finding a qualified buyer if we are open to negotiating part of the total as a trade rather than for cash.

In terms of trading one property for another, with cash added on one side or the other, this may be old hat. Yet in terms of bartering other things than real estate as a means of getting control of a property, the barter technique is only recently blooming into an entire segment of the real estate field.

"For every buyer with cash for a down payment, I can show you a hundred that have equity for a down payment," say Robert W. Steele in his *Fifty Ways To Buy or Sell a House.*[1] Equity, of

---

[1] Bob Steele is an active real estate exchanger, and conducts seminars on the subject throughout the country. See Appendix 2 for details of his other books and publisher's address.

159

course, can mean ownership—or a share of ownership—of real estate *or anything else.*

The most obvious alternative to cash, in the minds of the average members of trade clubs, is the organization's scrip—its trade dollars. Let's start there.

Avoid the "100 Percent Trade" Hustlers

Trade clubs vary greatly, because of the differing policies their managements lay down for the membership, how these policies are enforced, and the composition of the memberships themselves. Most are worthwhile and genuinely benefit their members, as noted in Chapter 3. Yet around the edges of even conservatively run trade organizations there sometimes appear specialists in real estate hustling. They may not even be members of any trade club, yet they can and do accept club credits and lay them off again to others who are members.

Vacant land which is owned free and clear (f/c) is, in itself, a kind of currency. Much the same as the millstone-sized stones once used on the island of Yap as its currency, such land changes hands as often as it can be traded or—occasionally—sold. It is a store of value, even if the owner of record at any moment has never seen it and never will.

Subdivision lots, especially small ones in undesirable communities, are the nickels and dimes of this currency land. Usually (not always, of course) this is the kind of land offered to the perhaps unsophisticated trade-club member who wants to convert his few thousand trade dollars into "a real estate investment."

Many members of trade clubs are professionals or small-business owners who gradually accumulate more trade dollars than they spend. Having neither the time, inclination, nor ability to become full-fledged traders, they look at their store of credits and long to invest them in something secure, such as land.

Playing up to these desires, there are a number of real estate brokers who offer some of their f/c-currency real estate to members of trade clubs at 100 percent trade credits. This is generally the least desirable portion of the broker's portfolio. He may well have taken it as "boot" in some other transaction. If he could have turned it easily in the cash marketplace he would have done so.

The broker offers his lots or acreage without ever having seen the land himself. He is thus not required to make the usual full disclosure; hence any bad features (suspected perhaps, but unverified) are not revealed to the club member whose desire to turn his credits into an investment often outweighs his otherwise good sense. So he lays down his few thousand units, gets his deed (almost invariably *not* a warranty deed!) and then eventually begins to wonder what to do with his property.

If he tries to sell it, or trade it for another piece of property, he will lack the sales flair of the broker who sold it to him. Any serious investor, unpressured by a desire to unload his dollars, will want to get an appraisal on the property even if he does not visit it himself.

You can use your own experience in real estate to imagine the kinds of flaws there might be in raw land—especially if subdivided—of this kind. It may be landlocked and without access, for example. It may be vertical instead of horizontal. It may be butted against an oil tank farm or an industrial plant whose fumes still violate antipollution regulations. The property may be under water. There may be no utilities available. Such defects are going to make the land virtually unsaleable except to another innocent, or as one of perhaps several pieces of property conveyed as a package in some larger-scale transaction.

If the club member should go to visit his land after he has bought it, and learns the actual details of its situation, he is then in the unenviable position of being required to reveal the negatives to any prospective purchaser. That's when the going gets really tough![2]

If you are getting into a trade club, and want to use the credits in part as investment potential in real estate, then read the next sections of this chapter.

Trading for the Down

Although this is written from the point of view of the prospective buyer, if you're the holder of real property and want to facilitate its sale, use these ideas to help your prospects turn into actual purchasers.

The inflation of recent years, together with the nation's growing population and other factors, has caused the price of real estate to rise steadily in all parts of the country. Forest land, grazing land, farm acreage, industrial or residential land, it has all been appreciating remarkably in terms of current dollars.

[2] Here's an interesting instance of this kind of property I turned up in the course of my research for this book. I investigated and inspected a subdivision lot in a small county-seat city in the state of Washington. The lot was being offered on the basis of 4,000 trade-club dollars, with no cash required. I looked up its location in the courthouse records, checked with the assessor's office, finally went out and saw the lot itself. Its legal description referred to it as the "westerly portion" of another lot; its dimensions in actuality were something on the order of 50′ × 40′ × 60′ × 30′, since it was the rhomboid end of the larger lot remaindered by the slashthrough of a street at an angle. "It's unbuildable," the clerk in the assessor's office told me, "because it's outside the city sewer lines, and it is too small to put in a drain-field for a septic tank. But that doesn't mean that it's unsaleable." True enough, if bought without investigation. My research revealed these further facts: it was carried on the county's books at $100, and that county assesses at 100 percent valuation. The taxes were $1.60 a year (which in this case is exactly the tax rate base). The lot had last changed hands four years before, consideration $1,000. This one little story contains just about all the plot elements you will find in the oft-repeated drama of the overeager buyer and the supersuave city-slicker seller. Pay heed, unless you don't mind role-playing in this sort of playlet yourself.

Under such conditions, the key to turning a profit in real estate is to *control* it. In some cases that can be done with an option; it can almost always be accomplished with a down payment that gets the buyer into it. Remembering Bob Steele's maxim, it becomes almost imperative that a prospective buyer utilize his equity in other things to come up with the down. Then he will occupy the property, lease or rent it, option it to someone else, or simply let it lie vacant (if land) until his tax adviser and the local market make it appropriate to sell. As long as appreciation continues, profits are built in and almost guaranteed.

If you are active in real estate now, or intend to be, make trading other things than money part of your modus operandi. You will extend the reach of your dollars tremendously, and will also make possible transactions which otherwise would never occur.

The first and most obvious place to start with your trading tactics is with the listing broker, if there is one, on the property you are concerned with. Get him to trade for his commission. This automatically cuts the amount of cash you need for a down payment, because the broker's fee comes out of that.

The full run of things you can use as trade goods is as broad as there are things with value. Bob Steele mentions some of them in his books, but we can develop the beginnings of a list without consulting anyone's text.

Begin with real estate itself. Mortgages, deeds of trust, options, and leases are all potential trade goods. Property held free and clear, or encumbered, is a prime valuable. So is a building to be moved, condominium or time-shared condo, mobile home, or even a trailer or travel home.

Any kind of automotive equipment, especially the more expensive kinds, can be proferred as trade merchandise in real estate deals.

Harry Reid, a trade broker in Los Angeles, was recently written up in *National Jeweler* because of his success in arranging trades of diamonds and other gem stones for real estate. Harry told me that the ease with which such deals can be put together is "unreal."

Barbara Thompson, a realtor in Tacoma, recently reported that one of her clients was able to pay 100 percent of the cost of membership in a time-sharing condominium club using trade credits of a leading barter group.

Stamps and coins of real value are also prime trading stock in real estate transactions these days. Stocks, bonds, and the expected proceeds from inheritances still in probate are also fine for trading in real-property acquisitions.

Extend this list as far as your ingenuity can take it.

The American Real Estate Exchange Market

In recent years real estate exchanging has expanded so greatly that there are groups in most parts of the country which exist for the sole purpose of providing brokers with a place and time to meet with their fellows to work out mutually beneficial exchanges. This may involve the properties of clients, or their own broker-owned inventories.

Unless you have followed developments in this portion of the real estate business, you may be surprised at the tremendous volume of transactions generated by such means, and the great enthusiasm the meetings arouse among participating brokers.

For further information, write for details about seminars conducted by The Academy of Real Estate, 46 North Washington Square, Sarasota, Florida 33577. Also send $5.95 for a sample issue of *American Exchangor*, a periodical, 6360 South Tamiami Trail, Sarasota, Florida 33581.

Also get details of subscribing to the *Real Estate News Observer*, 5850 Avenida Encinas, Carlsbad, California 92008—

$24.00 per year. It regularly carries details of meetings of exchange groups in all parts of the country as well as much else of interest to the exchanger field.

Trading for Investment Property

Any of the trading techniques—or trade goods—useful in working out an exchange for a home or other small real estate holding are quite valid for transactions involving investment property. Mainly the scale is different; usually the parties involved are better heeled and more canny in the ways of real estate exchanging.

It is possible to use trade-club credits as the entire purchase price. Al Jibilian, Los Angeles trader, told me of a buy he made using only club credits. The property was several hundred acres of land in Montana, which Al intended to slice into smaller units and sell off to other buyers at a profit to himself. Al said that the only cash expended by him was the transaction fee he had to pay the trade club, plus a few hundreds of dollars to procure some high-quality camera and stereo gear which he used as boot.

Harry Reid became part-owner of a diamond mine from some of his diamonds-for-real estate transactions. (His share came in lieu of certain commissions due on trades he arranged.)

When John Mixer was head of the ITX trade organization in Inglewood, California, he and an associate were concocting a deal in which a group of the club's members were to pool their credits to make the down payment on a hotel in one of the desert towns in Southern California. It was discussed that the owner would take all credits as a starter; the continuing payments would be in cash, taken from current operating income. That particular deal apparently fell through, but the concept is valid.

In ordinary real estate transactions, cash and notes, mortgages, deeds of trust, and similar items are thought of first when buying for personal use or investing.

Trades of other properties as part of such transactions rank right along with the items named above.

Farther down the list are unrelated goods, such as boats, cars, trailers, and so on.

Yet it is common for lawyers, accountants, building designers and architects, contractors, and even advertising/public relations people to trade their *services* for a unit in a development, a share in a partnership ownership of a building, or for a condominium. It is also very common to trade services or goods for rentals of property.

It is also becoming more common to use trade dollars in a trade club to get into real estate ownership, whether to occupy or as an investment.

Need a Loan? Borrow from Your Trade Club!

If you are a member in good standing in a well-run trade club, and have gained a reputation for fair and willing trading, the easiest way to obtain funds to use for real estate investment is to borrow them from your trade club. Trade dollars, though more difficult to spend than U.S. dollars, are ever so much easier to obtain, whether you get them in the ordinary course of business or borrow them.

Naturally, the details will differ from club to club. The outline will be something like this:

Trade club managements live from the transaction fees and cash and/or trade dollars generated by members of their organization. Real estate deals generate large quantities of fees because the amounts of the sale/purchase are large. Club managements like to foster such exchanges. They profit from them.

Assuming that your reputation and credit standing are okay, approach your club management with the details of your purchase. Work out the best deal you can—in percentage or total fees—for the trade dollars you require.

Management will no doubt demand that you pay the transaction fees up front. (Don't object to this; mainstream cash lenders demand points off the top for arranging loans, too.)

Management will also demand surety for repayment. If the total you borrow is small, your signature may be enough. Larger amounts will require that you pledge property of some kind. You may have to give a deed of trust or a mortgage in order to obtain still larger sums.

If you negotiate well, though, you will no doubt be able to obtain the trade credits on more favorable interest rates than those you would have to pay for a cash loan of the same size. (You may knock off two or three points from the going cash rates.) Also, very likely you will be able to procure a larger trade-dollar loan than would be available in the cash marketplace.

Whether the interest will be paid in cash, or cash and trade, will depend on your particular negotiations. Repayment terms are also variable in accordance with what you and your lender work out together, but usually will come out of your normal flow of earnings of the club's trade units.

Too hard to buy a property with trade dollars? Talk to Al Jibilian! If you find yourself doubting, go back over the process in Appendix 3.

Watch Your Step—and Your Wallet!

Whether you are using cash dollars, trade dollars, or some other valuable as your trading/purchasing exchange medium, stay alert.

Frequently non-trader types who nonetheless join a trade club wind up with a few thousand of the club's credits, which they are too lazy, ignorant, or stubborn to use for regular business or personal requirements. The lure of "investment" may be all it takes for them to unload their hoard as part or all of a real estate parcel touted to them by a smooth-talking hustler. They buy sight unseen. They gladly transfer their credits. Then, as the realities emerge sometime later, they have someone to hate instead of the trade-club operators (who had been their previous particular devils).

"If fools went not to market, bad wares would not be sold," runs an old Spanish proverb. You can avoid all such difficulties by using the same prudence you would in any transaction involving factors previously not known to you. Here are a few suggestions:

- Even if you consider your trade credits (or other trade capital) to be of doubtful value, still act as if they were of full face value.
- Get all related facts into the open. This may involve personal inspection of the real estate in question as well as an appraisal. Run a title search. Insist on a warranty deed and a title guarantee. Make sure all assessments, encumbrances, and other negatives are revealed and understood (and acceptable to you).
- Make sure that the transaction is handled through proper escrow arrangement, or at the very least have your lawyer read and okay everything before you sign and pay. If you are being rushed into the deal, ask yourself whether you would say yes so easily if the consideration were "real" dollars rather than "trade" dollars. (They are *all* dollars to the extent that you can make them return a dollar's worth of value; you can get taken for cash, too.)
- Keep in mind that the best buys are ones you uncover by your own search, not those brought to you by someone else.

Now Walk through This Again, Please

- Equity in something else is easier to come up with than cash, when you wish to buy real estate, so offer to trade it as part of the deal.

- Trade-club scrip is the closest thing to cash you are likely to have in abundant supply. Plan to use it.
- Just because you have saved, or can borrow, a substantial sum in trade dollars, don't get taken in by the real estate hustlers on the fringes of the marketplace who will try to sell your marginal "currency" properties.
- *Control* of property is the name of the game in real estate these days, with appreciation working in favor of the one in control.
- You can use trade credits or other valuable goods to get into property—by purchase or by option, or lease with option. You may even be able to use trade values to help pay for it on a continuing basis.
- Get into the habit of thinking outside the "normal," narrow, dollars-only channels when planning a real estate acquisition.
- Read some of the periodicals in the real estate exchange field.
- You may be able to get a trade-dollar loan from your trade club, and at less interest than you would have to pay for a cash loan.
- Some clever traders use trade-club credits for virtually 100 percent of the payment for sizeable investment properties.
- Others use their professional services to acquire real estate, in lieu of down payment or—in some instances—for full ownership of a share, a unit or a house.

A fair exchange is no robbery.   —*Smollett*

CHAPTER 13

Long Profits for You from Trade Fairs

NOT ALL TRADE CLUBS hold periodic trade fairs, open only to their own members and families. Many do. If you join one trade club you may well affiliate with two or three. Most trade clubbers seem to hold multiple memberships. Out of these several memberships, let's hope you will be able to attend—and sell at—such a gathering.

Once I was president of a mutually owned trade club named Fair Traders. We staged quarterly fairs for our group, with a fabulous turnout about two times a year, and a good attendance the other times. Trading was always good enough so that buying members could lay away gifts for Christmas, or replenish the stocks of various commodities, or buy on impulse for trade credits what they might not have picked up for cash.

Exhibitors enjoyed a fine traffic if their wares were intriguing, useful, and good values. The club itself benefitted both from the fees it collected on transactions and from the reawakened enthusiasm of members in attendance.

The fun and profit from a good trade-club fair is something I hope you will be able to experience for yourself. Seek it out if you do not have it brought to your door by your own club or clubs.

Naturally, you'll have to pay heed to the rules established by your particular club. Still, there are general points to keep in mind no matter what your club rules may be.

Planning to Sell?
Here's an Important Checklist

Merchandise. Select what you intend to sell with an eye to public buying preferences. Having observed what items were popular at trade fairs staged by four different trade clubs over a period of years, I found these categories of items generally attracting crowds of buyers: Jewelry · Tools · Clothing · Home Furnishings · Small Appliances · Artists' Works · Cameras · Watches · Calculators · Audio Gear · Stationery Products · Art Materials. (These are not listed in order of demand, nor does this exhaust the list of items that move well at trade fairs.)

Exhibit. Do as a good merchant does: choose a booth location with a good traffic flow. Set up necessary cases, racks, shelves, tables. Light it to enhance your merchandise.

Pricing. If the merchandise is from your regular stocks, of course you will maintain your normal pricing. If you have obtained the goods especially for selling at the fair, though, then price it competitively with what equivalent items bring in the cash marketplace. (If you don't, you will not attract other traders to buy from you.)

One hundred-per cent trade? Your club may require all transactions to be at full trade, with no cash involved. If so, you'll have to offer your goods that way. Even if your club will permit charging part cash, if you want to get maximum trade at your booth you'll still price yourself at 100 percent trade. (Every extra bit of cash required from a potential trade-club buyer adds to his or her reluctance to conclude the deal with you.)

Arrange for sales help. There's invariably a slowdown at the cashier's spot in trade-fair booths. Checks have to be made out, or vouchers filled in. Usually credit has to be cleared and purchases okayed. All this means delay. Several heads and pairs of hands will make it easier for you to show and discuss your goods *and* take care of the paperwork too. That will make it easier for you to increase your sales during the usual few hours of trade-fair selling.

Mr. Retailer, Clear Out Those Odds and Ends

While the thronging crowds of shoppers at a trade fair are not complete idiots, and will not snap up absurd offerings at outrageous prices, still there is some of the urge to spend typical of fairs and carnivals in general. Often the proud paterfamilias will take his wife and youngsters to the festivities, eager to show them what wonderful things he can buy for them by using only those magical trade dollars he has told them about, but which very likely they have never before helped him spend. Then too, trade fairs attract many of the less able traders, who manage to accumulate a store of trade credits but who apparently lack the time or skill necessary to keep them spent in the normal course of business. Trade fairs also attract expert traders, always on the lookout to purchase for trade dollars items they need or desire which otherwise they'd have to buy for cash.

All these kinds of traders make a trade fair a good place for a merchant to clear out his odd-lot assortments of merchandise. For instance, most traders will not demur to purchase goods at a trade fair simply because they are last year's models, or were closed out by the manufacturer, or are available only in broken sizes, styles, or colors.

If you are a retailer, keep setting aside special lots of items as the date for a trade fair draws near. Go a step further if you feel like it. Tap your wholesalers or manufacturers for special merchandise of the kind you judge will be attractive to trade fair attendees.

You may be able to obtain full retail in trade dollars for things which, if left in your store, you'd have to mark down drastically to move for cash. You may gain an extra margin of profit also from special buys which you pick up at reduced cost. Either way, assuming that you have set up regular channels for spending the trade dollars you take in, you will come out with a very profitable few hours of selling at a trade fair.

Long-Profit Tips for Service Operators

Many persons who operate service businesses take in old models of the equipment they sell in order to consummate transactions. Put into good working shape, such older pieces of machinery, for example, find a steady market in the cash marketplace—and they move quite readily at trade fairs.

I have seen service and repair specialists exhibiting at trade fairs such routine equipment as vacuum cleaners, sewing machines, cameras, motion-picture cameras and projectors, television and radio sets, adding machines and calculators, manual and electric typewriters, and office copiers.

Since by and large the only investment these exhibitors had in the things they were selling was the labor to bring them up to good working standards, they stood to make a very long profit on whatever they sold.

A side benefit for these service people who exhibit at trade fairs is that they have a chance to showcase themselves to a large number of other traders. This tends to bring them a continued flow of trade business over the months that follow a fair.

Some who are in service businesses, or even run professional practices, avail themselves of trade-fair sales opportunities to make continuing contacts, as well as to sell something that may not be related at all to their normal line.

I can recall a lawyer, for instance, who for years sold stationery products at trade fairs. He bought these at closeout sales and auctions at a few cents on the dollar. His profits were long indeed.

A distributor of feature films would be hard put to trade these off to trade-club members at a trade fair, but I know one such person who very successfully sold costume jewelry at handsome markups at trade fairs. He specialized in turquoise and Hawaiian puka necklaces and earrings.

Then there was the manager of one trade club who offered an exciting line of imported Indian artifacts—bracelets, pins, rings and brooches. He moved a lot of it, too, because it was fresh to the market and had not even been offered through usual channels for cash purchase.

A printer packaged up shrink-wrapped bundles of memo pads and sold them easily. (He cagily intermixed pads with different colors of paper stock, so they appealed to fashion-conscious women shoppers.)

A music school director sold used musical instruments, and in addition sold gift certificates good for a course of lessons.

Even a chiropractor I recall offered certificates good for a series of therapeutic massages. An optometrist featured an exhibit of reading/magnifying glasses, opera and field glasses, cleansers, and wipes.

Do you get the picture? Even if you are not normally a retailer, you can still act like one at a trade fair. Brainstorm it, when the chance comes your way. You can have a lot of fun and pick up a fat wad of trade credits too.

Artful Craftsmen Clean Up Big

I have observed only two reasons why some exhibiting artists do not sell their handiwork at a trade-club fair. Either the work is poor—it does not attract potential purchasers—or it is vastly overpriced.

Notice that I said *vastly overpriced*. That is because good work sells at trade-club fairs even if it is *somewhat* overpriced. Trade-club members are usually not quite so stingy in spending trade dollars as they would be with cash; then too art is a subjective commodity as well as a tangible, objective one, and a high price is a relative thing.

If your work finds ready buyers in galleries, open-air exhibits, or your own studio, you can expect a good sale at a trade fair. On the other hand, I have observed exhibitors bringing back the same tired and amateurish pieces trade fair after trade fair, seldom selling anything. The quality was simply not up to commercial standards.

Commercial standards, of course, have little to do with artistic standards, as any artist knows. But to be a successful vendor—for cash or trade dollars—requires production of objects generally accepted as of professional quality.

Good paintings and ceramics move better at trade fairs, in my experience, than do other things in the artsy-craftsy field. I have observed few buyers for stitchery items, little activity for wood or metal sculptures.

If you are a professional selling through galleries, you can take subjects that have been slow to sell when exhibited to cash purchasers and let them go for trade credits at full gallery prices. (A nice gain for you over what you'd usually get!)

If you are an amateur seeking professional standing, a trade-club fair may give you the equivalent of many profitable cash sales when you have as yet established no market for your work in the cash community.

If you are a rank beginner, or have no talent at all, the trade-club fair will do little for you beyond what the cash world has already done.

If You're Buying, Watch These Points

Quality of merchandise. As in any strange retailing situation, where odd-lot merchandise is being offered by dealers you do not know, pay close attention to the merchandise itself. Inspect clothing for those unstitched seams or dropped threads that indicate seconds. (Seconds may be all right for some uses, but not if you're being asked to pay full retail price for first-quality goods.)

On ceramics, crystal, or artistic bric-a-brac, make sure there are no chips, nicks, or cracks which would greatly reduce the value of the pieces.

If machinery or other mechanical devices are being sold as new, make certain by inspection that they show no evidence of prior use.

Use your own educated shopper's eye in general to be certain that sleazy materials and shoddy workmanship are not being palmed off at prices that would be acceptable only if the merchandise were of good quality.

Pricing. Assume that the goods are satisfactory: how about the price? If you are a buyer with eyes open in general, you will know without having to ask whether the price is high, just about fair, or represents a genuine bargain even for cash. (If you do not have such a well-taught sense of value, your education must begin somewhere. Much better that it should start with a few trade dollars at a trade fair than for many cash dollars somewhere else.) If you think the asking price is too high, there's nothing to prevent your offering a lesser amount, if you really would like the merchandise offered. Nor is there anything to stop you from simply moving on without even trying to negotiate a better deal.

Cash to boot. Some trade clubs have a policy forbidding anyone to trade for anything less than 100 percent barter. Other clubs permit cash and trade dollars to be mixed, in varying proportions according to circumstances. Exhibitors and shoppers alike will be governed by the rules of the sponsoring club. Generally, though, the wise buyer will spend his trade-club credits with those exhibitors offering merchandise without any cash required; after all, why bother to have a trade club with *barter* the *raison d'être* if more or less cash creeps back in to dilute the purity of the barter ideal?

The surest way to discourage those who want cash as well as trade credits for what they are selling is simply to go elsewhere. Otherwise you will be subsidizing their acquisition cost of the merchandise at the minimum, or paying them a cash profit on goods acquired for trade credits at the maximum.

Guarantees. Merchandise moved for trade dollars will ideally have the same guarantee of quality and serviceability as if sold for cash. Still it is up to you, as the buyer, to make certain you know the merchant's name and store address, since a trade fair is an impermanent location. You will also wish to get both a verbal assurance and a written guarantee on the kinds of mechanical or electronic devices that generally carry them. The warranty of the dealer is required, too, on used equipment he has refurbished and is reselling at the fair.

How's That Again?

- Trade-club fairs are good fun and can be profitable. Attend them whenever you can.
- If exhibiting, select merchandise generally appealing to the buying public, set up your booth so merchandise is displayed to advantage, price things at popular levels, get help in handling the paperwork.
- If you're a retailer, a trade-club fair can be a good chance to sell goods otherwise somewhat difficult to move at full price in your store.
- If you're in a service business, sell rebuilt equipment, or even offer wares not in your general business line.

- As an artist or craftsman, offer your good quality work at its full retail value (instead of the reduced price you'd get if a gallery operator had sold it for you and taken off his markup).
- In buying at a trade-club fair make sure first that the merchandise is satisfactory in quality. Then judge whether the price is a reasonable one. Think twice about buying if the vendor wants cash in addition to trade credits. Assure yourself that the goods you buy carry normal guarantees, such as you would obtain as a matter of course if buying for cash.

APPENDICES

Active U.S. Trade Clubs

THIS IS NOT A COMPLETE LIST of trade clubs in the United States. My research for this book has not revealed any really compendious list of such groups. The one you see here is revised and expanded markedly from the only other extant list that came to hand. As I see it, there are two main reasons for the nonexistence of accurate and full lists of trade clubs. One is that it's a volatile segment of American business. New groups spring up here and there, around the country, almost every week. There's always a lag between when the club is organized and the time it is publicly in existence in phone books or other directories. The largest trade-club organizations are national in scope, and are actively franchising. New branches or affiliates are being opened in almost every important city in the nation. The same lag exists here, except that it is caused by the difficulty in getting accurate data out of the national home offices.

Trade clubs also die, or have their membership absorbed by larger and more viable groups. (Three disappeared within the past few months in the Los Angeles area alone, for instance.) Lists of any great age are thus going to be markedly out of touch with the actual facts.

Another reason for the lack of accurate lists of trade clubs is the fact that, as a group, the clubs don't fit into any of the standard directory categories. Look under "Trade" for trade clubs in the Yellow Pages, for instance, and you are invited to consult "Business & Trade Organizations." All right: under *that* heading in the Seattle directory, the one closest to hand, may be seen only two groups—the Better Business Bureau and a plumbing industry trust. Period.

Let's try another tack. How about listings under *Barter*. Well, between Bartender Schools and Baseball Clubs (where Barter ought to be) there is no listing.

Okay, but what about *Financial* headings? No luck again. Under *Financial Planning Consultants*, no barter groups. Same with *Financial Public Relations Counselors, Financing*, and *Financing Consultants*. That ends the *Financial* classifications, and *still* no trade clubs can be found in the Seattle Yellow Pages.[1]

All three of the country's largest national trade-club systems have active offices in the Seattle metropolitan area, with an aggregate membership of perhaps 1,500 traders. Yet unless you already know them by name, it's hard to locate their offices.

All of this is a preface to the carefully assembled but still incomplete listings which follow. If you do not find a club office in your area, call one or two nearby offices and ask about your local community. There may be a club there already, known to those in the trade-club business. If so, they will generally be glad to provide the information you are seeking.

[1] The same nonlisting occurs also under *Clubs* and *Organizations*. Try your own Yellow Pages to see if you can do better.

NATIONAL TRADE CLUBS

Business Exchange, Inc. (called BX in the trade)
International Headquarters
4716 Vineland Avenue
North Hollywood, California 91602
(213) 877-2161 or 984-1233

Costs: $195 to join; $36 annually. Cash charge on purchases 8 percent; no trade percentage deducted. Transactions are carried out by predenominated computer-generated checks, updated with value stamps issued each month. Most exchanging is done at 100 percent trade; however, larger purchases may be at negotiable percentages of cash as well as trade credits. Issues a directory.

Business Exchange offices:

BX/Mobile
132-D Du Rhu Drive
Mobile, AL 36608
(205) 344-3292

BX/Arizona
8071 Via Del Deserto
Scottsdale, AZ 85258
(602) 991-9227

BX/San Gabriel Valley
2406 W. Valley Blvd.
Alhambra, CA 91803
(213) 283-3002

BX/Downey/Long Beach
16446 S. Woodruff
Bellflower, CA 90706
(213) 920-8896

BX/NorCal
41580 Fremont Blvd.
Fremont, CA 94538
(415) 656-1570

BX/Santa Barbara
P.O. Box 1358
Goleta, CA 93017
(805) 967-9543

BX/San Bernardino/Riverside
7153 Park Blvd.
Joshua Tree, CA 92252
(714) 366-2634

BX/West Los Angeles
8622 Bellanca Avenue
Los Angeles, CA 90045
(213) 641-5620

BX/Ventura County
P.O. Box 6224
Oxnard, CA 93031
  (805) 659-0714

BX/San Diego
7341 Clairmont Drive
San Diego, CA 92111
  (714) 268-3441

BX/Orange County
505 North Tustin Suite 221
Santa Ana, CA 92705
  (714) 973-1712

BX/Ottawa/Hull
2544 Sheffield Road
Ottawa, Ont., Canada K1B 3V7
  (613) 744-1410

BX/Toronto
3535 Lakeshore Blvd., W.
Toronto, Ont., Canada M8W 1P4
  (416) 259-1680

BX/Jacksonville
2121 Corporate Square Blvd.
  Suite 111
Jacksonville, FL 32216
  (904) 725-3931

BX/Georgia, Inc.
P.O. Box 12144
Atlanta, GA 30355
  (404) 237-7660

BX/Spokane
3207 Lodgepole Road
Coeur d'Alene, ID 83814
  (208) 667-8960

BX/Northern Illinois, Inc.
1124 3rd Avenue #2
7th Street Annex Bldg.
Rockford, IL 61104
  (815) 962-6611

BX/Indiana
7829 W. Washington
Indianapolis, IN 46231
  (317) 247-5191

BX/Des Moines
5359 NW 72nd Street
Des Moines, Iowa 50301
  (712) 278-2387

BX/Maine
44 Center Street
Bangor, ME 04401
  (207) 942-6316

BX/New Hampshire
Piscataqua Street
New Castle, NH 03854
  (603) 436-6674

BX/Massachusetts
48 Congress Street   First
  Management
Portsmouth, NH 03801
  (603) 431-7755

BX/ New Jersey
298 Greenway Rd.
Ridgewood, NJ 07450
  (201) 447-1317

BX/New Mexico
12209 Kinley Ave., NE
Albuquerque, NM 87112
(505) 296-5507

BX/Western New York
12 Main Street
Hamburg, NY 14075
(716) 648-1400

BX/of the Carolinas, Inc.
311 S. Main Street
Kernersville, NC 27284
(919) 996-5921

BX/Oklahoma City
2012 N. McArthur
Oklahoma City, OK 73127
(405) 942-7812

BX/Portland
12311 S.E. Division
Portland, OR 97236
(503) 239-4607

BX/Eastern Tennessee
Route 20—Emory Road
Knoxville, TN 37921

BX/International of Dallas
6929 Vista Willow
Dallas, TX 75248
(214) 661-8978

BX/Longview/Tyler
800 Aledo
Longview, TX 75604

BX/Utah
316 South 4th East
Salt Lake City, UT 84111
(801) 364-4365

BX/Seattle
Koll Business Ctr., 570 Industry
Dr.
Seattle, WA 98188
(206) 575-4183

Exchange Enterprises
159 West Haven Avenue
Salt Lake City, Utah 84115
(801) 487-1641

Costs: $25 to join plus $175 annual dues paid in advance. No fees to sellers; 10 percent trade fee charges collected from buyers. Publishes no directory: member calls office, states need, is directed to another member who has the desired merchandise or service. Exchange is effected by means of buyer's identification card. Trades are at full retail prices, 100 percent barter.

Exchange Enterprises offices:

Mr. Chuck Wheeler
P. O. Box 41976
Anchorage, AK 99509

Mr. Dick McGhan
2111 E. Broadway
Tempe, AZ 85282

Mr. Frank Spindler
2/381 High Street Road
Mt. Waverley, Victoria 3149
Melbourne, Australia

Mr. Wallace Parker
2940 Randolph Ave.
Costa Mesa, CA 92626

Mr. A. LeRoy Atkins
6657 Sungrove St.
Garden Grove, CA 92640

Mr. Jay Lyon
1043 Stuart St. #6
Lafayette, CA 94549

Mr. Robert Roberts
8753 Broadway
LaMesa, CA 92041

Mr. Bruce Wattles
2331 El Camino Ave.
Sacramento, CA 95821

Mr. Bruce Galbraith
1030 The Alameda
San Jose, CA 95126

Mr. Jack McKinney
P. O. Box 8544
Stockton, CA 95208

Mr. Rex Baldwin
4715 Kippling
Wheatridge, CO 80033

Mr. Don Sa'aga
P. O. Box 27083
Honolulu, HI 96827

Mr. Wayne Holladay
347 C Street
Idaho Falls, ID 83401

Mr. Tracy Wright
P. O. Box 685
Meridian, ID 83642

Mr. William Nicholes
P. O. Box 1951
Twin Falls, ID 83301

Mr. Charles Kincaid
4645 Executive Dr.
Columbus, OH 43220

Mr. Box Onken
1843 State St.
Plaza Bldg.
Bettendorf, IA 52722

Mr. Jerry Evenson
4108 Lincoln Road
Missoula, MT 59801

Mr. Judd Wagner
13706 Shongaska
Omaha, NB 86112

Mr. James Maxwell
1721 E. Charleston Blvd.
Suite 19
Las Vegas, NV 89104

Mr. Neil Baker
P. O. Box 7495
Reno, NV 89510

Mr. Joseph Wood
11105 Menaul N. E.
Albuquerque, NM 87123

Mr. Larry Inks
4848 No. MacArthur
Oklahoma City, OK 73122

Mr. Jay Whiting
11125 N. E. Sandy Blvd.
Portland, OR 97220

Mr. Elliott Roberts
13999 Goldmark
Dallas, TX 75240

Mr. David Dehlin
P. O. Box 19648
Houston, TX 77024

Mr. Steven Van Luven
P. O. Box 3625
Bellevue, WA 98009

Mr. Kenneth Haueter
East 209 Sprague
Spokane, WA 99202

Mr. Jeff Christensen
P. O. Box 1081
Tacoma, WA 98401

International Trade Exchange
7656 Burford Drive
McLean, Virginia 22101
(703) 821–1101

You do not join ITE directly, but rather become a member of an affiliated club and pay an annual fee for intercity exchange privileges with other ITE clubs. Cost of individual club membership appears to vary: $150 to $200 seems the range of prices. $100 additional pays for ITE privileges. Trade fees vary somewhat between clubs, too: 10 percent all cash in most; with 10 percent half cash, half trade also noted. This list, dated March 27, 1979, was supplied by International Trade Exchange headquarters. However, some clubs included here indicated on questionnaires returned by them separately that they are *not* members of ITE. In such instances they have been listed here as well as under the Independent Trade Clubs heading.

International Trade Exchange affiliated clubs:

Arkansas Trade Exchange
11121 North Rodney Parham
Little Rock, AR 72212

New England Trade Exchange
1 Padanaram Road '115
Danbury, CT 06810

Connecticut Trade Exchange
700 Burnside Avenue
East Hartford, CT 06108

Central Florida Trade Exchange
508 Orange Drive #2
Altamonate Springs, FL 32701

ITE of Broward County/Palm
  Beach
2440 East Commercial
  Boulevard
Ft. Lauderd)le, FL 33310

Florida Trade Exchange
3100 University Boulevard South
Jacksonville, FL 32216

Gulf Coast Trade Exchange
P. O. Box 8125
Pensacola, FL 32505

Greater Atlanta Trade Exchange
2219 Perimeter Center East
Atlanta, GA 30346

Midwest Trade Exchange
2650 N. Lakeview Drive #2701
Chicago, IL 60614

Northern Illinois Trade
  Exchange
1806 South Alpine
Rockford, IL 61108

ITE of Indiana
537 Turtle Creek S. Drive #10
Indianapolis, IN 46227

Greater Iowa Trade Exchange
Equitable Building #812
Des Moines, IA 50309

ITE of Omaha
5717 Hickman Road
Des Moines, IA 50310

Wichita Trade Exchange
8210 North Oliver
Valley Center, KS 67147

Kentucky Trade Exchange
129 Briarwood Road
Versailles, KY 40383

Lake Charles Trade Exchange
P. O. Box 5915
Lake Charles, LA 70606

New Orleans Trade Exchange
7303 Downman Road
New Orleans, LA 70126

Ark-La-Tex Trade Exchange
P. O. Box 5763
Shreveport, LA 71105

Portland Trade Exchange
980 Forest Avenue
Portland, ME 04103

Worcester Trade Exchange
57 Cedar Street
Worcester, MA 01609

Michigan Trade Exchange
29246 Van Dyke
Warren, MI 48093

Twin Cities Trade Exchange
(Consult telephone information
or ITE headquarters for address)

Jackson Trade Exchange
1755 Lelia Drive #102
Jackson, MS 39216

New Hampshire Trade Exchange
RFD 1, Box 151
Auburn, NH 03032

Philadelphia Trade Exchange
U.S. Route 130
Burlington, NJ 18016

Trade Exchange of New Jersey
77 Milltown Road
East Brunswick, NJ 08816

Tri-City Trade Exchange
1985 Central Avenue
Albany, NY 12205

Rochester Trade Exchange
16 West Main Street #438
Rochester, NY 14614

Western New York Trade
Exchange
3095 Elmwood Avenue
Town of Tonawanda, NY 14217

Trade Exchange of North
Carolina
926 Second Street N.E.
Hickory, NC 28601

Cincinnati Trade Exchange
11413-A Century Boulevard
Cincinnati, OH 45246

Dayton Trade Exchange
1150 Richfield Center Road
Dayton, OH 45246

Toledo Trade Exchange
121-1/2 West Indiana Avenue
Perrysburg, OH 43551

ITE of East. Ohio & West. Pa.
821 Dollar Bank Building
Youngstown, OH 44503

Central Pennsylvania Trade
Exchange
P.O. Box 2637
Harrisburg, PA 17105

Delaware Valley Trade Exchange
1150 1st Avenue #410
King of Prussia, PA 19506

Tri-State Trade Exchange
603 Fairway Drive
West Chester, PA 19380

South Carolina Trade Exchange
P. O. Box 12452
Columbia, SC 29211

Nashville Trade Exchange
No. 2 Maryland Farms #339
Brentwood, TN 37027

East Tennessee Trade Exchange
P. O. Box 26
Sweetwater, TN 37874

High Plains Trade Exchange
724 S. Polk Street #901
Amarillo, TX 79101

Dallas/Ft. Worth Trade
   Exchange
5019 N. McKinney #130
Dallas, TX 75205

Western Trade Exchange
1855 Trawood Avenue #E
El Paso, TX 79935

West Texas Trade Exchange
7212 Joliet Street #3-B
Lubbock, TX 79423

Austin Trade Exchange
6836 San Pedro Road South
   #105
San Antonio, TX 78216

San Antonio Trade Exchange
6836 San Pedro Road South
   #105
San Antonio, TX 78216

Virginia Trade Exchange
1631 Old Virginia Beach Road
   #B
Virginia Beach, VA 23453

Mutual Credit
6300 Variel St.
Woodland Hills, CA 91367
(213) 703-6500

A rapidly growing trade club which, while still actively promoting exchanges among its members, is developing into a unique financial service company. Cost to join: $300 deposit (credited to member's account in trade dollars). Transaction fees: 8 percent cash on purchases, 5 percent trade on sales. Members who agree to automatic deduction of fees from bank account, or debit on Bank Charge or other major credit card, have privilege of accepting cash-business charges on both major cards from the general public and barter and barter/cash charges from other members. Members may lease phone-connected instrument for electronic credit clearance on all cash or barter sales, plus immediate collection/deposit of all trade or cash funds. Mutual Credit members are categorized by percentage trade: *25, 50, 75, 100.*

Mutual Credit offices:

Mutual Credit—Alaska Regional #101
Post Office Box 3-3888
Anchorage, AK 99501
UPS: 926 East Fourth
Anchorage, AK 99501
John Hendrickson, Jim Seacord
& Bob Chopp
(907) 272-7125 (o)
(907) 272-5262 (h) Jim Seacord
(907) 333-0507 (h) Bob Chopp

Mutual Credit—Arizona Regional #44
1600 W. Camelback, Suite 2-N
Phoenix, AZ 85015
Jerry Laurie, Ruth Laurie and
Emil Kohn
(602) 266-6137

Mutual Credit—Phoenix Regional
5651 N. 7th Street #101
Phoenix, AZ 85014

Mutual Credit—Tucson Office
4021 E. Grant Road, Suite 3
Tucson, AZ 85711
Bob Nuis
(602) 236-8134 (h)
(602) 881-6913 (o)

Mutual Credit—British Columbia Regional
14692 111th Avenue
Surrey, B.C., Canada

Mutual Credit—Canada National Office #86
421 King Street North
Waterloo, Ontario N2J 4E4
Brian W. Turnbull
(519) 886-7810 (o)

Mutual Credit—Santa Clara Regional
1901 S. Bascom #334, The Towers
Campbell, CA 95008

Mutual Credit—Sacramento Regional—#50
P. O. Box 418
Concord, CA 94522
UPS: 1903 Queen's Road
Concord, Ca.
Bob Biesecker
(415) 676-3555

Mutual Credit—River City Service Center #77
1540 River Park Drive, Suite 105
Sacramento, CA 95815
Jack Lomax
(916) 920-4412
(916) 920-0444

Mutual Credit—San Francisco
  Regional #40
P. O. Box 418
Concord, CA 94522
UPS: 1903 Queen's Rd.
  Concord, CA
Bob Biesecker
(415) 676-3555

Mutual Credit—Fresno Regional
P. O. Box 26386
Fresno, CA 93704

Mutual Credit—Orange Co. W.
  Regional
13169 Brookhurst #A
Garden Grove, CA 92643

Mutual Credit—Marin Branch
851 Scown Lane
Novato, CA 94947

Mutual Credit—Venice Branch
  #222
723 Ocean Front Walk
Venice, CA 90291
Sol Genuth
(213) 392-8318

Mutual Credit—Ventura Branch
  #38
141 Sawtelle Avenue
Oxnard, CA 93030
Derek DeBacker
(805) 985-1472

Mutual Credit—Ventura
  Regional
2889 West 5th Street
Oxnard, CA 93030

Mutual Credit—Riverside
  Branch #216
3590 Central Avenue, Suite 202
Riverside, CA 92506
Lee Burnett and Sharon
  Tucevich
(714) 784-3931
(714) 784-3934

Mutual Credit—San Diego
  Regional
3526 Fairmount
San Diego, CA 92105

Mutual Credit—Peninsula
  Branch
P. O. Box 3217
San Mateo, CA 94403

Mutual Credit—Peninsula Service Center #68
290 Winchester Court
Foster City, CA 94404
Jack Burket
(415) 573-6225

Mutual Credit—Santa Rosa Service Center #4
50 Santa Rosa Avenue
Crocker Bank Building—Room
  280
Santa Rosa, CA 95404
Cecil N. Self
(707) 523-4242 (o)
(707) 544-1754 (h)

Mutual Credit—Tahoe Branch
P. O. Drawer 7046
Tahoe City, CA 95730

Mutual Credit—Tahoe Branch
P. O. Box 11762
Tahoe Paradise, CA 95708

Mutual Credit—North Bay
Branch
1510 Sears Point Road
Vallejo, CA 94590

Mutual Credit—Colorado Regional Office #89
6475 Wadsworth Blvd., Suite 114
Arvada, CO 80003
Ken Marquardt
(303) 424-0062 (o)
(303) 423-5699 (h)

Mutual Credit—Arvada Branch #8
6475 Wadsworth Blvd., Suite 114
Arvada, CO 80003
Elmer Neff Jr.
(303) 424-6440

Mutual Credit—Colorado Springs Branch #83
715 Circle Drive, Suite 102
Colorado Springs, CO 80910
Robert Post
(303) 635-5945

Mutual Credit—Southeast Denver Branch
2250 South Onida #200
Denver, CO 80222

Mutual Credit—Fort Collins Branch #203
1552 Riverside
Fort Collins, CO 80524
Art Pforr
(303) 493-3634

Mutual Credit—Mile Hi Branch #22
48 Steele St., Suite 200
Denver, CO 80206
Ed and Evelyn Seeger
(303) 320-8406

Mutual Credit—Northglenn Branch
11842 McCrumb Drive
Northglenn, CO 80233

Mutual Credit—Denver Central Branch #12
3200 W. 71st Avenue, Unit 20
Westminster, CO 80030
Fred Jensen
(303) 427-3492

Mutual Credit—Westminster Branch
7255 Irving Street #209
Westminster, CO 80030

Mutual Credit—Brevard County Branch #76
600 North Courtney Drive
Merritt Island, FL 32952
Jack Trostorff
(305) 452-8880

Mutual Credit—Ft. Lauderdale
  Branch*

Mutual Credit—Lake Wales
  Branch #23
61-B Deland Avenue
Indian Lake Estates, FL 33855
Emanuel R. Cavallaro
(813) 692-1384 h
(813) 692-1045 o

Mutual Credit—Jacksonville
  Branch
2570 Atlantic Boulevard
Jacksonville, FL 32207

Mutual Credit—Florida Branch
  #43
P. O. Box 5456
Lakeland, FL 33803
Marc Perry
(813) 688-0811

Mutual Credit—Florida Regional
58 Lake Morton Drive
Lakeland, FL 33811

Mutual Credit—Florida Regional
Morton Professional Center
Lakeland, FL 33811

Mutual Credit—Lakeland Re-
  gional #51
P. O. Box 5456
Lakeland, FL 33803
UPS: 4610 Luce Road
     Lakeland, FL 33803
Marc Perry
(813) 688-0811

Mutual Credit—Lakeland
  Branch
117 South Florida Avenue
Lakeland, FL 33801

Mutual Credit—Orlando-Mait-
  land Branch
465 Stefanik Road
Maitland, FL 32751

Mutual Credit—Central Florida
  Branch #76
555 North U.S. 17–92
Casselberry, FL 32707
Roy Sampley
(305) 339–3322

Mutual Credit—Orlando Branch
  #63
2126-C West Oak Ridge
Orlando, FL 32809
Phillip Gottlieb
(305) 857–1636

Mutual Credit—Orlando Branch
7026 Tripoli Way
Orlando, FL 32807

Mutual Credit—St. Petersburg
  Branch #219
2580 East Bay Isle Drive S.E.
St. Petersburg, FL 33705
(813) 894–4459

* Office franchised but not yet open at press time. Call Regional Office or ask
Directory Assistance operator for telephone number.

Mutual Credit—Tampa Branch #48
P. O. Box 5456
Lakeland, FL 33803
Marc Perry
(813) 688-0811

Mutual Credit—Atlanta Branch
1320 North Lake Mall
Atlanta, GA 30345

Mutual Credit—Atlanta Regional #19
P. O. Box 720316
290 Hilderbrand, Suite #10A
Atlanta, GA 30328
Dave Arrowood
(404) 992-1259
(404) 993-0553 h

Mutual Credit—Greater Atlanta Branch #202
c/o Merle Norman Cosmetics
1320 North Lake Mall
Atlanta, GA 30345
Emilie and Richard Bishop
(404) 491-0093 o
(404) 491-8063 h

Mutual Credit—Capitol Branch #5
P. O. Box 12244
Atlanta, GA 30305
3177 Peachtree Drive North East
Atlanta, GA 30305
Jim Suttle & Bill Foltz
(404) 255-6011

Mutual Credit—Hawaii Regional #105
677 Ala Moana, Suite 410
Honolulu, HI 96813
Clyde Shields
(808) 521-5306

Mutual Credit—Maui Branch #210
Whalers Market Place
505 Front Street #32
Lahaina, Maui, HI 96761
J. West
(808) 667-6751
(808) 667-9184

Mutual Credit—Waikiki Branch #223
307 Lewers #404
Waikiki Beach, Honolulu, HI 96815
J. West
(808) 922-4936 o
(808) 395-7633

Mutual Credit—Idaho Regional #52
2309 Mountain View Dr., Suite 108
Boise, ID 83704
Paul Miletich
(208) 377-2519

Mutual Credit—Kansas Regional #106
125 North Main
P. O. Box 370
Hesston, KS 67062
William Dick
(316) 327-2782

Mutual Credit—Wichita Branch #204
566 S. Oliver, Suite B
Wichita, KS 67218
Leon Janzen
(316) 684-4702

Mutual Credit—Minnesota Regional
1522 University
St. Paul, MN 55104

Mutual Credit—Minnesota Regional #58
1533 University
St. Paul, MN 55104
Norville Pervier
(612) 644-8602

Mutual Credit—Jackson Branch
P. O. Box 808
Batesville, MS 38606

Mutual Credit—Carson City Branch #94
311 Kitchen Drive
Carson City, NV 89701
Norris R. Hinton
(702) 883-3721

Mutual Credit—Reno Branch*

Mutual Credit—Las Vegas Branch #3
3644 South Carrera Circle
Las Vegas, NV 89103
Al Faccinto Jr. and David Cox
(702) 871-5298

Mutual Credit—Nevada Regional #37
309 Wonder Street
Reno, NV 89502
Art and Karen Binford
(702) 329-4898

Mutual Credit—Newark
854 Poole Avenue
Hazlet, NJ 07730

Mutual Credit—Newark Service Center
12-16 Bank Street #7
Newark, NJ 07901

Mutual Credit—New York Western Regional
3407 Delaware Avenue
Buffalo, NY 14217

Mutual Credit—Niagara Falls Branch
826 Pine Avenue
Niagara Falls, NY 14301

Mutual Credit—New York Western Regional
1370 Niagara Falls Boulevard
Tonawanda, NY 14150

Mutual Credit—Charlotte Regional #103
4801 Independence Blvd., Suite 815
Charlotte, SC 28205
Jack Whitaker
(704) 535-4043

* Office franchised but not yet open at press time. Call Regional Office or ask Directory Assistance operator for telephone number.

Mutual Credit—Oklahoma
 Regional
1301 South Broadway, Suite 206
Edmond, OK 73034
Phil Watson
(405) 341-7372

Mutual Credit—Tulsa Regional
3010 South Harvard #302
Tulsa, OK 74114

Mutual Credit—Klamath Falls
 Branch
310 Bridge
Ashland, OR 97520
Donald & Judy Rist

Mutual Credit—Coos Bay
 Branch
525 S. 6th Street
Coos Bay, OR 97420
Kenneth Bigelow
(503) 267-4781

Mutual Credit—Corvallis Branch
 #96
2151 N.W. Fillmore
Corvallis, OR 97330
Ken Wright
(503) 754-0441

Mutual Credit—Oregon Pacific
 Branch
P. O. Box 1226
Newport, OR 97365
UPS: 229 N.E. 6th Street
 Newport, OR 97365
Tom Flansberg
(503) 265-6344

Mutual Credit—East Portland
 Branch
12200 N. Jantzen Avenue #125
Portland, OR 97217

Mutual Credit—East Portland
 Branch #72
P. O. Box 13500
Portland, OR 97213
UPS: 4436-B N.E. 131st Pl. &
 Sandy Blvd.
 Portland, OR 97230
Mac Sohlstrom & Andy Spuck
(503) 256-4444

Mutual Credit—Longview
 Branch #88
1906 Florida
Longview, WA 98632
Leo and Donna Mason
(206) 425-3038

Mutual Credit—Portland Branch
5319 S.S. Westgate Drive #150
Portland, OR 97221

Mutual Credit—Portland Metro
 Branch #74
P. O. Box 2905
Portland, OR 97208
UPS: 12340 N.W. Marshall
 Portland, OR 97229
Roy Jay
(503) 641-6189

Mutual Credit—Roseburg
 Branch #97
1333 S.E. Court Street
Roseburg, OR 97470
Eddie Parker and Ken Bokish
(503) 673-2733

Mutual Credit—Salem Office #60
3875 River Road North
Salem, OR 97303
Terry Wilson
(503) 390–1799

Mutual Credit—Roseburg Branch
780 N.W. Gleneagle Drive
Sherwood, OR 97140

Mutual Credit—Eugene/Springfield Branch #69
1505 N. 18th St., Suite C
Springfield, OR 97477
Hugh C. Barnwell
(503) 741–0241

Mutual Credit—Pendleton-Lagrande Branch #213
P. O. Box 1314
Pendleton, OR 97801
UPS: 1201 N.W. Cardin
    Pendleton, OR 97801
Darry Nelson, Mgr. for James King
(503) 276–4075

Mutual Credit—Greenville Regional #45
P. O. Box 5212
Greenville, SC 29606
UPS: 116 West Stone Avenue
    Greenville, SC 29609
Joe Shabkie and Lou Martin
(803) 242–1458

Mutual Credit—Myrtle Beach Branch #18
P. O. Box 332
Myrtle Beach, SC 29577
UPS: 3801 North Kings Hwy.
    Myrtle Beach, SC 29577
Thom Martin & B.J. Fuller
(803) 448–9483

Mutual Credit—Memphis Regional #55
2182 Gorham Place
Germantown, TN 38138
Eddie and Win Peterson
(901) 754–0853

Mutual Credit—East Memphis Branch #61
3099 Rising Sun Road
Memphis, TN 38134
Edward J. Rice
(901) 372–1706

Mutual Credit—Dallas-Fort Worth Regional #39
2925 LBJ Freeway, Suite 180
Dallas, TX 75234
Bill DuBois and Richard E. Davis
(214) 620–7262
(214) 596–6254 (h) Bill DuBois
(214) 980–9964 (h)   ”   ”
Mail: P. O. Box 1005
    Addison, Texas 75001

Mutual Credit—Jackson Mississippi Branch #208
3035 Directors Rd., Suite 416
Memphis, TN 38131
William & Betty Faulkner
(901) 345-2278
(601) 563-7885 (h)

Mutual Credit—Whitehaven #87
3035 Directors Rd., Suite 416
Memphis, TN 38131
William and Betty Faulkner
(901) 345-2278
(601) 563-7885 (h)

Mutual Credit—Dallas North Branch
5428-30 East Winton
Dallas, TX 75206

Mutual Credit—El Paso Regional
Manila Drive
El Paso, TX 79924

Mutual Credit—Houston Regional*

Mutual Credit—Tarrant County Regional
3628 Brentwood
Odessa, TX 79762

Mutual Credit—San Antonio Regional #218
7910 Rugged Ridge
San Antonio, TX 78250
Gene D. Cruson
(512) 681-4868

Mutual Credit—Utah Regional
7720 Brighton Way
Salt Lake City, UT 84121
Richard Henderson
(801) 943-0529

Mutual Credit—Bellingham #9
P. O. Box 1465
Bellingham, WA 98225
Charles P. and Annabelle J. Houglum
(206) 676-8431
UPS: 3734 D'Linda Street
Bellingham, WA 98225

Mutual Credit—Lewis County Branch
902 "E" Street
Centralia, WA 98531

Mutual Credit—Seattle-Tacoma Regional #57
30819-B Pacific Highway South
Federal Way, WA 98003
Richard and Valerie Cox
(206) 927-3725
(206) 941-0363

Mutual Credit—Longview Branch
1906 Florida
Longview, WA 98632

* Office franchised but not yet open at press time. Call Regional Office or ask Directory Assistance operator for telephone number.

Mutual Credit—Everett Branch
#93
2927 Rockefeller
Suite A
Everett, WA 98201
John Isley
(206) 258-6418
(206) 222-7753

Mutual Credit—Mount Vernon
Branch #28
P. O. Box 1271
Mount Vernon, WA 98273
UPS: 935 Talcott Street
Sedro-Wooley, WA 98284
George Burtt
(206) 424-0415
(206) 855-1952

Mutual Credit—Olympia Branch
#10
1301 N.E. 45th
Seattle, WA 98105
(206) 745-9533 (h)
(206) 633-2020 (o)
(206) 643-1050 (o)

Mutual Credit—Seattle Branch
#62
6328 22nd Avenue N.E.
Seattle, WA 98115
Garth Wallis
(206) 525-0177

Mutual Credit—Spokane Branch
#71
West 1625 Nebraska
Spokane, WA 99208
Leslye and Ron Olson
(509) 328-9995

Mutual Credit—North Pierce
Branch #212
515 Harvard Street
FirCrest, WA 98446
Derryl F. and Kay E. Harris
(206) 472-9205 (h)

Mutual Credit—Tacoma Branch
#29
12606 Bridgeport Way S.W.
Tacoma, WA 98499
Barbara Thompson
(206) 582-9100
(206) 582-7545

Mutual Credit—Tri City Branch
#225
627 North East Stephens
Roseburg, OR 97470
William and Debbie Tatum
(206) 582-9100
(206) 582-7545

Mutual Credit—Vancouver Regional #56
7407 N.E. Hiway 99, Suite C
Vancouver, WA 98665
Mike and Gay Lemmon
(206) 699-4550 (o)
(206) 573-5282 (h)

Mutual Credit—Lower Columbia Branch #90
7407 N.E. Hiway 99, Suite C
Vancouver, WA 98665
David B. Isabel, Albert K. Archer and Donald L. Wolfe
(206) 699-4550

Mutual Credit—Wisconsin Service Center
3801 West Vliet Street
Milwaukee, WI 53208

Mutual Credit—Wyoming Regional*

Mutual Credit—Bend Branch #7
P. O. Box 424
Gleneden Beach, OR 97388
Gary & Marilyn Nichols
(503) 994-8720

Mutual Credit—Grand Junction Branch*

Mutual Credit—Medford Branch #85
206 West 9th St.
Medford, OR 97501
Ken and Helen Poore
(503) 779-3158

Mutual Credit—Redding Branch*

Mutual Credit—Tri-Cities Branch*

INDEPENDENT TRADE CLUBS

Even the smallest of these independent trade clubs has more than 100 members. Most have memberships in the 300–500 range. The largest exceed 1,000 members. Many have exchange agreements with other leading independent clubs, so that arrangements of a satisfactory kind can be made to accommodate visiting members from out-of-city organizations. The large independent clubs, in some instances, have several offices within the same general geographical region.

Blue Key Exchange
851 Burlway Road #416
Burlingame, CA 94010

Trade Note Interchange
819 Eleventh Avenue
Delano, CA 93215

* Office franchised but not yet open at press time. Call Regional Office or ask Directory Assistance operator for telephone number.

TradeAmericard Corporation
777 South Main Street # 204
Orange, CA 92668

Trade Systems Corporation
4960 Hamilton Avenue
San Jose, CA 95130

United Trade Club
3031 Trisch Way
San Jose, CA 95100

North American Trade Exch. of
Denver, Inc.
6850 East Evans Avenue
Suite 140
Denver, CO 80224

Gulf Coast Trade Exchange, Inc.
P. O. Box 8125
Pensacola, FL 32505

Executive Trade Club
1000 Bishop Street
Honolulu, HI 96813

The Maine Trade Exchange
980 Forest Avenue
Portland, ME 04103

Business Owner's Exchange, Inc.
4901 West 77th Street #123-B
Minneapolis, MN 55435

Philadelphia Trade Exchange
Doyle Building, Route 130
Burlington, NJ 08016

American Reciprocal Trade Systems, Inc.
9 Northern Boulevard
Greenvale, NY 11548

American Reciprocal Trade Systems, Inc.
95 Madison Avenue
New York, NY 10016

Rochester Trade Exchange, Inc.
16 West Main Street #438
Rochester, NY 14614

American Barter Systems
Division of Area Barterers Inc.
170 East Post Road
White Plains, NY 10601

Columbus Trade Exchange
7870 Olentawgy River Road
Columbus, OH 43085

Central Pennsylvania Trade
Exchange
2233 N. Front Street
Harrisburg, PA 17105

Pittsburgh Trade Exchange
471 Lincoln Avenue
Pittsburgh, PA 15202

Tri-State Trade Exchange, Inc.
603 Fairway Drive
West Chester, PA 19380

East Tennesssee Exchange
P. O. Box 26
Sweetwater, TN 37874

Unlimited Business Exchange
3471 South West Temple
Salt Lake City, UT 84115

Barter Americard
2973 Bond Drive
Merrick, NY 11566

National Commerce Exchange
6501 Loisdale Road
Springfield, VA 22150

Directories and Sources

THIS ADD-ON SECTION is not intended to answer all your questions about Who and Where in trading. Rather, its purpose is to head you in certain directions which, if followed in your own way, should reveal the exact kinds of information and sources you desire to locate.

A primary source of information, convenient to nearly all of us, is a good public library. All libraries of the kind, no matter how small, have reference sections or departments. The larger libraries have separate business sections.

For information sources in the form of periodicals and directories, ask at the reference desk to see the current edition of *Standard Periodical Directory*. It is separated into sections, each devoted to some particular general topic or interest. It lists essential information on the thousands of publications in the United States of interest to one segment or another of the public. It is published by Oxbridge Communications, Inc., 1345 Avenue of the Americas, New York, NY 10019.

Your reference librarian can direct you to other directories of possible interest to you, too. Talk over your needs with her or him.

A second source of help—and one with a lot of leverage built in—is your representative in Congress. (If you don't know his name, or how to reach him, ask your librarian to let you see the current *Congressional Directory.*) Your congressman will have a field office or two near you. You can talk to a staff member there and explain what you would like to find out (or obtain) from the federal government. Someone will go to work on the matter and see that you are attended to.

What you think the government can supply is your business. The standard item is *information*—where and how to get government contracts, assistance, grants, and so forth. The congressman's staff in Washington knows the way the government machine works, and exerts leverage on your behalf. You as a voter, and an influence in the district back home, have leverage as against the congressman and his staff, who depend on your good will and support to stay in office. Bureaucrats, whose budgets must be voted by Congress, are consequently leveraged by the congressional staff. See how it works?

You may have specific needs for your business. The Department of Commerce has experts on both exporting and importing to help you. (They'll even give you reports on foreign firms you intend to do business with.) The Small Business Administration also offers plenty of help, including backing loans. You can find field offices for both Commerce and SBA in some of our larger cities, or contact Washington directly.

If you have interest in importing or exporting to/from specific countries, get in touch with the commercial attachés at their consulates—also in our larger cities, especially ports of entry. U.S. consular offices abroad can also assist you in those same nations.

It's not my intent to steer you to export-import contacts unduly, though that aspect of business can provide enormous profit opportunity. Yet while we are on that subject, if the field interests you, be sure to obtain a sample copy ($4.00) of *The Monthly Ex.Im. Opportunities*, listing hundreds of detailed offerings and wants from/by companies in all parts of the world. Dr. Paul B. Singer, the publisher, also has other services and books. Address: P.O. Box 1033, Station "C," Scarborough, Ontario, Canada M1G 3T2.

Or you might want to procure *International Drop Shipment Directory* or *American Importers Directory*, each $5.00, from P.O. Box 454, Hollywood, CA 90028. Still another directory of value, providing sources of promotion help from import sources and exporters, is *Importers & Exporters Trade Promotion Guide*, published by World Wide Trade Service, P.O. Box 283, Medina, WA 98039. A sample issue is $5.00.

If surplus or recycled merchandise should interest you, your congressman's staffer contact can steer you to U.S. government surplus sales. In addition, major corporations sell off unwanted used equipment in various ways. A phone call to the public relations office of any one near you will clue you as to whether there's an opportunity for you there—to buy low, refurbish, sell high. You might want to look over a copy of *Surplus Dealers Directory*. Including the *Bulletin*, a monthly publication, it costs $10, and is available from the Institute of Surplus Dealers, Inc., 520 Broadway, New York, NY 10012.

Perhaps real estate appeals to you as a good entrance to trading in an important way. Then by all means be in touch with Newport Book & Seminar Company, P.O. Box 1554, Medford, OR 97501. They publish the highly creative real estate trading books written by Robert W. Steele, and arrange his seminars. Ask for what information you wish. *American Exchangor*, 6360 S. Tamiami Trail, Sarasota, FL 33581, is devoted to the subject of exchanging as applied to real estate. Sample copy is $5.95. Also write The Academy of Real Estate, 46 N. Washington Square,

Sarasota, FL 33577, for information about their programs of continuing education for real estate people and investors. The Academy can also provide information about Charles G. Possick's seminars on the exchanging of personal property; or write Possick in care of Synergetic Marketing Corp., 10629 Bay Pines Blvd., St. Petersburg, FL 33708.

If you'd like to exchange real estate for diamonds or other gems, be in touch with Harry Reid, American Exchange, 7250 Franklin Avenue, Penthouse, Los Angeles, CA 90046.

Maybe you have sizeable quantities of products you manufacture which you'd like to convert into something else. Or you may have radio or television commercial availabilities, or hotel/motel rooms, or restaurant meals, or something similar which you'd like to turn into profit. Then you may wish to contact a reciprocal trader. Send $5.00 for a sample issue of *Barter Communique*, published by Full Circle Marketing Corp., 6500 Midnight Pass Road, Penthouse Suite 504, Sarasota, FL 33581. Robert Murley, who heads the operation, is an expert in arranging trades for both ends of the exchange process. ALL Advertising Associates, 18 Madonna Blvd., St. Petersburg, FL 33715, is another high-volume reciprocal trader. (It's recommended that you don't bother any of these people unless you are sincere and have at least a few thousand dollars' worth of merchantable goods or services to trade.) There are scores of other trading firms in the United States, large and small; you will find out how to reach them as you energetically expand your own barter horizons by seeking smaller trades to begin with.

If you wish to get expert advice and many services free (in exchange for occasionally rendering such services yourself) you will do well to get in touch with Richard Johnson, Free-for-All, 1623 Granville, Los Angeles, CA 90025. The group now numbers many hundreds of experts in many fields (including law, accounting, psychology, etc.) and you are able to call upon these *mavens* as freely as you desire, within the limits of time the organization's rules permit. At latest word membership is $15 initiation plus $11 annual dues; you receive a membership directory listing all the services provided by each member. Since the original core of Free-for-All was a special-interest group of the high-IQ society, Mensa, its experts tend to be really expert.

If you intend to join a trade club, check out the special services members get in Mutual Credit, 6300 Variel St., Woodland Hills, CA 91367. While barter on an indirect basis was the original catalyst of the organization, members currently have other things going for them, which aid them in the cash community. Mutual Credit members can clear credit on VISA or Master Charge cards, for example, and if they subscribe to the extra service can have a computer terminal connected to a phone line in their place of business; it clears *and collects* funds on these cards in a thirty-second transaction. The same method clears credit on Mutual Credit members' barter accounts. Tied in with the system is a nationwide check-guarantee plan; another part of the Mutual Credit program is a 10 per cent discount card recently introduced to the general public, good at Mutual Credit members' establishments, and back by the cardholder's other credit cards. (The merchant is reimbursed by Mutual Credit in the operation.)

Maybe you are interested in starting a trade club of your own. If so, be sure to see or talk with Michael Ames, head of Trade-Americard in Orange, California. Mike invites entrepreneurial types to spend a couple of weeks in his office (for a fee), learning everything he knows about the business. Reach him at Trade Americard, 777 South Main Street, #204, Orange, CA 92668.

Effective Ways of Changing Aspects of Your Personality

SOME YEARS AGO, IN ANOTHER BOOK OF MINE—*Stop Crying at Your Own Movies*—I went into great detail to explain the theory and practice of altering one's undesired habit patterns. Although the book is still in print,[1] this brief discussion and instructions will point you in the correct direction for shaping yourself up for more effective exchanging.

The methods used have been tested by many counselors, on many hundreds of their counselees, for many years. They can work with what seems almost miraculous ease and speed and effectiveness.

The human personality is something like a combination lock. You can fiddle around with it long enough and you may, without knowing how, manage to unlock the thing. You happened to hit the right combination.

But if you possess the master combination, then unlocking any particular lock can be fairly easy. The formula given here is such a master combination.

Before we get to that, however, let's say that there are at least

[1] Nelson-Hall Company, 325 W. Jackson Blvd., Chicago, IL 60606

two other ways of getting rid of an undesired specific behavior pattern.

One is to wear it out by repeated demonstration that it is not applicable. Toastmasters groups, which take trembling would-be speechmakers and *insist* that they get to their feet and talk every meeting, use this sort of technique. The same method is used in father-son training sessions, in which the father *enforces* the son's personal fisticuffs with the neighborhood bully so that he learns that he *can* after all stand up for himself.

But this method usually requires that someone outside ourselves stand over us and keep us heading into the unpleasant task again and again, until, finally, we get the message that we *can* do it (whatever it is) with freedom and perhaps even pleasure. Frequently, we will duck out of situations in which we might be forced to do this sort of thing. As a result, the method is not very widely applicable.

Another way to deal with such personality-problem areas is to wait for the gradual amelioration that time brings, or for the sudden release which may come at any moment for no reason we are aware of. But this method is not too desirable, either, because it may or may not work for us. Only time will tell. Meanwhile, we are stuck with whatever the difficulty is we'd like to change.

Professional counselors use many approaches, from aversion therapy to simple listening, to help their clients straighten out what they (the clients) are complaining about. But the batting average of these professionals, by and large, is not very good when it comes to singling out and eliminating very specific annoying or limiting habits or beliefs.

The method that follows assumes that the personality is not just one massive chunk, but is made up of pieces. These pieces provide the particular formulas for action—or reaction—in challenges which we have stuck in place from time to time throughout our lives.

These individual action patterns are created when we *know*

that something is *true*. This knowledge is frequently not absorbed by our conscious awareness at the time the "knowing" takes place. Later, we may be aware that our patterned response does not make good sense, but we still go through with it time after time.

The steps to take in order to dismantle any particular old "truth" about self, others, life, or anything else, are these:

1. **Look for the pattern in your current life situation**, and state the "truth" behind it. A single thought usually sums it up. Phrases such as these occur frequently in setting up such truths:

"Whenever I . . . then I . . ."   "The world is . . ."
"I always . . ."   "People are . . ."
"Each time I . . ."   "I have to . . ."
"They always . . ."   "I never can . . ."

2. **Cast your mind back to the first time** such a thing happened (remembered, recalled in vivid detail, conjectured or imagined are all equally okay). Note how the response pattern still bothering you has continued ever since that early point in your life.

3. **Be aware of the emotion or emotions** accompanying the thought in the pattern. Look for emotions such as:

Apathy	Antagonism
Grief	Pain
Guilt	Irritation
Shame	Boredom
Fear	Interest
Resentment	Enthusiasm
Hate	Exhilaration
Rage	Joy

Along with the emotion will go certain stresses in the body, attempts the body made *to do something* when the original emotion was present. So:

4. **Observe the stresses in your body** present in the original experience (and replayed now each time the pattern is re-evoked). Look for stresses accompanying the attempt (for example):

To strike out	To wrench free
To flee, hide, or disappear	To expand or contract
To succumb	To get rid of something
To freeze, hold still, wait	To hold on to something

Do not limit yourself to these typical stresses, given for purposes of illustration only. Pinpoint the precise stress or stresses present in your body back then when the first incident occurred.

Also note the general conditions of your life and surroundings at the original period: illness, accident, emotional shock, anesthesia, drugs . . . also changes occurring due to puberty, injury, etc.

And be aware of the sense of "always," which seems to pervade childhood, as well as the value of the "truth" in your life. (What does it let you do, or keep you from having to do; what does it prevent from happening, or make it easier to have happen, etc.?)

Isolate these elements one by one. As you do so, *make the physical gesture* of taking them out of your body and throwing them away, as you tick them off:

This is the *thought* from the truth I got out of that early incident . . . I can certainly let it go . . . here it goes! (Toss it away.)

Here's the *emotion* . . . out it goes! (Throw it away.)

And the *stresses* that accompany that emotion . . . away with them! (Discarding motion.)

Continue with the "always," the value, the sense of general conditions, and so on.

If necessary, do it twice. If that hasn't eliminated the pattern so it *feels okay* when you look it over, see if you've overlooked some key element. If so, get rid of *that*. Or check to see if you have really been dealing with the *first* such instance in your life. If not, do the routine with that other, earlier occurrence.

You can use this formula on *compulsive* habits, on *phobias*, on generalized *attitudes* with equivalent success. It works as well on light, minor items as it goes on serious, heavy ones.

Once gone, the patterns typically stay gone. Just like that.

There is no need to replace the old pattern with anything else. You will find you now have the freedom to respond in some more suitable way, in the area of your life previously limited to just that one narrow reaction. The freedom even includes the ability to do the same old dumb thing again, if that's the best thing to do at the moment. (But that rarely is the case.)